Backyard Farming

Growing Your Own Fresh Vegetables, Fruits, and Herbs in a Small Space

by
Lee Foster

CHRONICLE BOOKS · SAN FRANCISCO

To Anke

Library of Congress Cataloging in Publication Data
Foster, Lee, 1943–
  Backyard farming.

  (Urban life series ; 2)
  1. Vegetable gardening.   2. Organic gardening.
3. Fruit-culture.   I. Title.   II. Series.
SB324.3.F67   635   81-4449
ISBN 0-87701-224-5   AACR2

Editing by Sylvia E. Stein.
Book and cover design by Drake Jordan.
Composition by Dharma Press.
Illustrations by Shirley Barker.
Cover photography by Howard Campbell.

Chronicle Books
870 Market Street
San Francisco, CA 94102

Table of Contents

Introduction

In 1976 I considered whether it would be possible to grow all the vegetables for my family on our modest-sized lot in Oakland, California. I wondered what amount of country-style food production I could achieve in the urban area, where I wanted to remain, where most of us are destined to live.

You may have thought along similar lines: What can I grow in my apartment? How many vegetables can I produce on my city lot? Or, with all this suburban space, can't our family produce much of its own food? You may have already started. A recent Gallup poll survey concludes that thirty-four million American households do some food gardening.

Within two years, I am happy to report, I was growing *all* the vegetables, most of the herbs, and much of the fruit for myself and my family. If invited to lunch at our place, you would experience the following.

We begin with a salad of our favorite lettuce, Oak Leaf, add succulent cherry tomatoes from a sprawling Sweet 100 plant and cucumbers of the variety called Saladin, and top it with a dressing of vinegar, oil, and our own herbs (basil, rosemary, oregano, parsley, and garlic).

We proceed to an omclet whose base is our own sauteed shallots and whose top is a garnish of our Sugar Snap peas and sprigs of fresh dill.

For dessert, we choose from a bowl of freshly picked strawberries. The luscious taste of strawberries has escaped you if you've eaten only the supermarket product, even at its best.

We're able to maintain this good eating year-round, with seasonal variations in the vegetables offered. This good living is within your range, too. Compare my situation a few years back with your condition today. I had no skills in vegetable gardening. Our city lot is not large, only 55 by 100 feet, but perched on a corner, with the house centered. Our chief asset is a strong sun, year-round, since we are located on a hill facing south. Our microclimate is frost free.

Your own tale of food gardening can be a success story if you begin slowly and persevere. Let me offer our evolution for inspira-

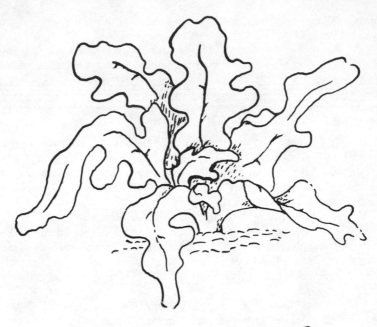

OAK LEAF LETTUCE

tion. Picture yourself here, realizing that you don't have to accept the ideal of growing *all* your own vegetables. Start small and advance your production as you meet success.

I began slowly with two tomato plants, plus lettuce and onions for salads. Through the first year and a half I devoted an hour a day to developing our soil and acquiring the skills and information needed. Our area, called Rockridge, is well named for its hard soil. At a composting site near the Berkeley city dump, where all the city tree clippings were shredded and composted, I bought ample amounts of organic material to improve the structure and nutritive levels of my soil. Eventually my own composting systems managed our vegetative wastes and helped sustain our vegetables' nutritional needs.

By late in the first year, most of my raised beds were completed. Raised beds are simply wood frames defining a garden area of loose, elevated soil. Raised beds keep foot traffic from compressing the growing grounds. I made the beds 5 by 10 feet. I erected a fence to keep out roaming dogs from the 900 square feet of sunny land that I finally reclaimed. The space proved sufficient, by the end of the second year, to make us self-reliant for vegetables.

At that point the full pleasures and rationale of the vegetable garden were apparent. Each evening we ate a different fresh vegetable. Young beets had an appealing taste that surpassed what a market could offer. The gourmet in me began to assert itself: How good to have a supply of fresh basil for pesto sauce. How delightful to relish fresh picked pole beans right off the vine. How pleasant to consume large, plump peaches ripened on the tree. Many of my food tastes had atrophied because they had not recently been excited by such quality food.

Our cauliflower had none of the pesticide residue laced on most commercial produce. What better way to arrange for pure food than grow it myself? Using integrated pest control techniques, I learned to avoid all pest poisons. The use of pesticides in California has risen from 56 million pounds in 1974 to over 111 million pounds per year today. That's more than 4 pounds for every man, woman, and child in the state, plus a good dosage for fish and wildlife. A home garden can be a small sanctuary and a reasonable alternative in such a situation. With the medical projection that one of four Americans alive today will contract some form of cancer, the time has come for a reasonable person to reduce the risk from one contributor, pesticides.

We developed a fondness for tender varieties of vegetables, such as endive, rarely available in our markets. The criterion for my plantings was "How does it taste?" rather than "Is it tough enough to ship?" Each vegetable has numerous varieties that can be grown by the home gardener, but would not withstand commercial shipping.

Our spinach came to table at its nutritive and cosmetic peak rather than deteriorated and wilted from the days that pass between picking and eating. Our children found it congenial to eat such vegetables because they were fresh, crisp, succulent, and attractive.

We grew broccoli with a minimum of fossil fuel costs. Our largest fossil fuel expenditure involved importing water, but studies estimate that the home gardener in our area can grow a pound of broccoli for about 12 percent of the water used by commercial growers. I don't have to saturate a furrowed field to get critical water to my plants in our semidesert climate. I avoid the high fossil fuel energy costs that our society pays for fertilizers, farm machinery operation, processing, transporting food to distant markets, and then carting the food from market to house. One study concludes that the energy costs of the home gardener are one one-hundredth that of conventional commercial agriculture.

We enlivened food with our own herbs and hot peppers, reducing dependence on salt as flavoring.

While living out the joys of eating foods we had grown, we also began to experience long-range economies in our food budget, 20 percent of the average American's living expense. The cost of fresh vegetables continues to increase faster than income. The trend is bound to continue as our conventional agriculture, entirely dependent on fossil fuels, passes on to consumers the rising costs of these depletable energy sources. My current production is worth about $1500 tax free per year in market prices, though the comparison is never fair because my own food is superior to the market produce in taste, appearance, variety of types, absence of poisons, and nutriments from picking immediately before consumption, at the peak of ripeness.

Some other subtle benefits began to emerge from our food gardening. We found that the other food gardeners we met contrasted with the typical urban person. The food producers seemed to be happier about their lives. They controlled more of their life. They were less vulnerable to prices fixed by remote businesses. They felt more self-reliant. They understood better the rhythms of nature and the need to flow with them. They were tanned and trim from the wholesome sun and exercise of their gardens. They seemed less alienated than other urban folk because from start to finish they controlled some of the food products they consumed.

I wanted more exercise but didn't want to jog. Gardening helped, especially on those rigorous days when the soil needed to be turned at major transition times in the growing cycle.

Some effects of urban food growing were unexpected. On December 22, when the angle of the vegetable-vitalizing sun began to rise after sinking to its nadir, I was ready to celebrate the return of light and life to the world. This enduring thread of primitive tradition gave a meaning to Christmas that no theological claim or quibble could violate. I appreciated as never before the wisdom of cultures that worshipped the sun.

Vegetable gardening made the backyard a zoo, bringing before me, my wife Anke, and our children a colorful range of insect wildlife. From my first accidental encounter with a mature praying mantis up close, eyeball to eyeball, I will always remember this beneficial insect's monstrous aspect. Ecology became something more than a learned abstraction when the interdependence of the garden confronted us.

Food production also bound our family together, with everyone assigned roles and all watching in surprise as a squash plant poked its head out one day and grew a foot the next day in hot July weather. Temperature changes, prospective rains, and powerful winds became dynamic rather than passive presences in our lives.

Occasionally I yearned for more space. But on other days the parameters of my small space vegetable garden became a satisfying limit. Knowing the boundaries of my property, I wondered with what ingenuity I could develop this space for maximum production. The efficient use of this space is part of the larger mental adjustment of our time, making small beautiful, expanding inwardly rather than outwardly, cultivating and conserving rather than pioneering.

As our food-producing systems grew more complex, with composting and drip irrigation, vegetable gardening defied a tenet of geometry: The whole was greater than the sum of the parts.

1: Maximize Your Minimum Space

Where to Food Garden

If you are a homeowner with access to ground space, you will have more opportunities than an apartment dweller to food garden. However, even an apartment balcony can produce substantial amounts of vegetables and herbs. Also, two million Americans now participate in community gardens. For information on containers and community gardens, see Chapter 6. In this chapter I consider gardening in the ground at your own homesite.

Growing vegetables in the ground rather than in containers has several advantages. The ground is a large reservoir for water, more protective of plant roots that dry out quickly in containers when weather is hot and windy. Ground temperatures vary less than those of container soil. The soil complexity of the ground can also work in your favor, allowing the free migration of earthworms to increase the aeration of roots. If you can get access to the ground, start there.

The Edible Landscape

Food production in the city requires a subtle but pervasive shift in landscaping values, adding together the concepts edible and ornamental to create an edible, ornamental landscape.

Part of the nearly 19 million acres of showy lawn space in the United States could be used for vegetable growing. Food production in confined urban areas also encourages us to abandon our somewhat luxurious sense of space and concentrate on intense use of each square foot.

The front of my house has been transformed in this direction. Below the front picture window are three Red and Yellow Delicious apple trees trained on wooden trellises, with Tioga strawberries at their base, and artichoke plants next to the sidewalk. To the left and right of the front steps are red currant bushes. On the other side of the steps is a large almond tree, with strawberries around its base, and a Blenheim apricot trained against the wall.

In spring the sea of blossoms from the almond, apple, and apricot trees is a lovely sight, especially as the bees work them over. In

AN EDIBLE LANDSCAPE

summer the greenery is attractive. Throughout the summer and autumn I eat off this landscape. I also maintain ornamental flowers in this area because of their beauty and because they boost the population of small wasps that keep pests, such as aphids, in check. The wasps need constant nectar supplies from flowering plants to maintain a large population.

For an edible landscape, you might consider other plants. In front of a house the herb basil, all kinds of peppers, and eggplant make attractive summer borders. The tall sunflowerlike stalks of Jerusalem artichokes are a satisfactory barrier and develop tasty tuberous roots. New Zealand spinach offers a pronounced greenery and nutritious, edible leaves. I even use a small type of tree, called a tree collard, as a barrier on one part of my side vegetable garden. The tree collard has attractive, purple, edible leaves.

Asparagus, artichokes, and rhubarb are perennials to consider for border areas.

Dwarf rootstock fruit trees are good choices of food-bearing trees. I now have seven such trees on my property. Dwarf rootstock keeps the tree to 15 feet or lower. The size of the fruit is standard, not dwarf.

In some situations a long-term investment in a full-sized fruit or nut tree may be possible. Fortunately for me, the previous owner of my house, who had a passing interest in food gardening, planted an avocado and a plum tree in the backyard years ago. For the first ten years he never saw an avocado and harvested only a few plums. Today I harvest an amazing six hundred to fifteen hundred avocados each year and anywhere from four hundred to twelve hundred plums. It takes an act of imagination for you to picture what a large tree would look like ten years from now. Be sure to evaluate how its shadow line will fall, considering the high angle of the sun in summer and the low angle in winter.

Good Food-Growing Spaces

Access to sunlight is the first criterion for evaluating your potential food-growing spaces. Leafy vegetables will grow reasonably well in moderate shade, but vegetables whose fruit or seed we eat, such as tomatoes, beans, and squash, will need six to eight hours of sunlight per day. If you have a climate that permits spring and autumn gardening, be sure to consider the sun angle at those times, when the sun is low in the sky and may be blocked by buildings or trees.

You may want to make some landscape changes to reduce obstacles to sunlight. I removed an unloved juniper tree near the front of my property because it blocked autumn and spring sun from about 200 square feet of my raised beds.

Convenient water delivery is another factor. Make long-range plans for a simple but flexible hose and soaker system. Put in plenty of Y-valves between beds so you can deliver water where you want it. You may want the onions to dry out, but the carrots need to be kept moist.

Wind protection may also be a consideration in discovering your gardening space. If wind is a problem, what could you erect as an edible barrier? Perhaps a constantly changing fence of beans and peas or a wire espalier of dwarf fruit trees. You may be able to produce some of your own wind-stopping lumber, as I do, with fast-growing bamboo. My bamboo stakes are now 1 inch in diameter, after about five years. They are excellent lumber for climbing plants and smaller staked plants. The invasive roots of the bamboo require constant checking, however.

Raised Bed Garden Space

Once you have decided where to plant, I strongly suggest defining the area with raised beds. I make my beds 5 by 10 feet, when possible, so I have easy access to all parts of the bed. For the defining boards I buy recycled lumber, from 1-by-8 to 2-by-12 doug fir or other species. Recycled lumber suppliers can be found in the Yellow Pages under "Lumber, Used." I coat all the boards with a nontoxic linseed oil and mineral spirits product, called Behr Gloss, to give them added life.

Raised beds serve several purposes. They determine where I will walk and where the plant roots will grow. Once the area has been defined, consider it sacred and never allow it to be compressed with foot traffic again. Raised beds also keep children, dogs, and cats moving along pathways and out of the growing area. After a couple of years of digging the area as deeply as possible with organic material, the soil will be soft, crumbly, and well aerated, requiring little further tilling, only a constant top dressing of compost. A raised bed with much organic material holds water well but allows it to drain. Raised beds warm up quickly in the spring. They are easy to tend, with less stooping, because of their slight elevation.

I cover the pathways between beds with bark chips or sawdust, which can be obtained free as the sawn waste at local lumber stores or cabinet shops. The sawdust keeps my boots clean in rainy weather. Sawdust also composts gradually and becomes part of the soil, but before decomposition the high carbon content in sawdust starves possible weeds on paths by using all available nitrogen. Snails and slugs don't like to migrate across sawdust because it irritates their mucous membranes. Sawdust also retains rainwater on my property rather than allowing it to wash into the sewers. Using sawdust in this manner turns a waste into a resource, part of the general philosophy behind much urban food gardening.

For walking around garden space, I recommend getting loose-fitting, sturdy, all-weather rubber boots you can easily slip your feet in and out of. I get mine at surplus stores for about $15. By wearing the boots in the garden and then leaving them at the door, I never track mud into the house. When you've poured a glass of wine and prepared a few crackers with cheese and someone says, "Why don't you get some chive from your garden for these cheese crackers?" and you look outside and see the rain coming down, you're more likely

MAXIMIZE VERTICAL GROWING SPACE

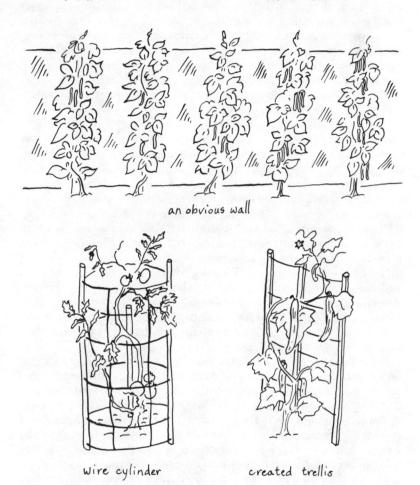

an obvious wall

wire cylinder   created trellis

to get the chive if you can slip easily into boots. If not, you'll judge it's not worth the effort and miss a garden pleasure you're entitled to.

Vertical Growing Space

When you're planning your food-growing space, vertical space can be even more useful to you than horizontal space. In warm weather, Kentucky Wonder pole beans and Big Boy tomatoes trained in wire cages produce handsomely in my garden. Cucumbers are another climber. In the cool season, I use the same area for Sugar Snap peas or Melting Pod Chinese snow peas. I have even trained warm-weather zucchini and yellow crookneck squash to grow vertically in wire cages, disciplining the plants by tying the vines to the cage. Considering the square footage invested, vertical climbing plants are the heaviest producers in my garden.

Analyze first what obvious vertical spaces you have. Then determine what other vertical spaces you could create, perhaps permanently, with frames of 2-by-2 lumber and wire.

An existing sunny wall presents a good vertical growing opportunity. Walls and fences may allow you to espalier fruit trees. When the sun is high overhead in summer, walls that couldn't be used in winter because of shade become productive growing space.

The racks and cylinders you create present many additional vertical growing spaces. For example, I have one 5-by-10 bed in the backyard that gets good sun in summer. I could use the space to grow bush beans with some success. But by installing 8-foot-high 2-by-2 posts at the four corners and then 2-by-2 spans between them, I have remarkable additional growing space. I plant the back and sides to beans and use the sun-sheltered interior for summer lettuce and spinach, which would bolt if exposed to constant sun but thrive in the filtered and blocked summer sun at the interior of the bed. I use the same arrangement for climbing peas in the cool autumn and spring seasons.

When using vertical space for peas and beans, I often grow them on twine rather than on concrete reinforcing wire. Twine works well for tendril plants because at the end of the season I can cut the twine and toss the entire bundle into the compost pile, where the twine will decompose along with the vegetation. The twine I use is hennequin from the Yucatan. This saves me the tedious task of cleaning all the vine tendrils and stalks that encircle wire. All these plant leftovers must be removed from wire or pests winter over and damage future crops. Buy twine in quantity or you'll be nickeled and dimed to death. I buy a large ball, enough to last a year, for about $5.

Unused Space

Your property may have large spaces not used for foot traffic or for pleasurable family activity. A large space along the side of my house fits this description. The area was lawn, adjacent to sidewalk. A large bougainvillaea bush prevented access to the area from the backyard, which my family used heavily. Periodically I had to go around the bougainvillaea bush and mow the grass. When the space

RECLAIMED HILL SPACE

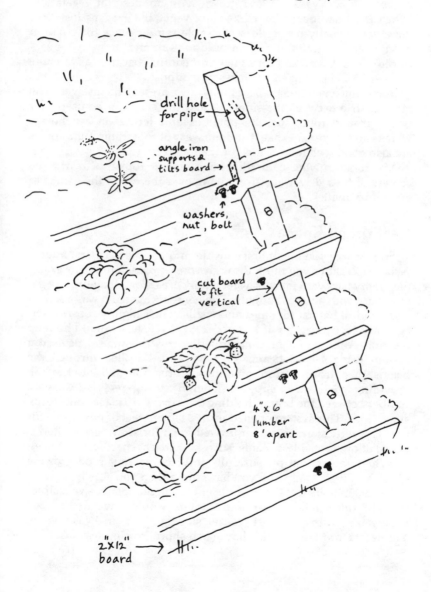

drill hole for pipe→

angle iron supports & tilts board →

↑
washers, nut, bolt

cut board to fit vertical →

4"x 6" lumber 8' apart

2"x12" → board

was fenced in and a doorway cut through the bougainvillaea, this space provided an excellent food garden terrain.

When you begin to think about what space you could use for food production, the amount available may amaze you. I discovered that half of my backyard was overgrown with nondescript vegetation. When it all had been cleared and my vegetable gardens installed, there was actually no net loss in usable family space for children playing or for adults having an outdoor summer dinner. We sacrificed little lawn, and the lawn remaining became a valuable "harvest" of clippings for mulches or compost.

Some unconventional spaces may also present themselves. The median strip between the sidewalk and the curb can be useful for below-ground food, such as potatoes and Jerusalem artichokes, which can escape car exhaust and the wear of foot traffic. Sunflowers are also good seed food plants for the median strip.

My food-growing comrades have staked tomatoes down the centers of their driveways after giving over the use of the garage to nonauto activities.

Reclaimed Space

Some space you might first consider impossible may later appear reclaimable, after you think through your approach to it. For example, in my backyard there is a steep hilly area. For a long time I eyed this space with hostile thoughts. The ivy that covered it was a retreat and an ideal habitat for slugs and snails. Their nightly forays damaged my vegetables. But if I ripped out the ivy, how could I hold up the hill? After a year of contemplating this dilemma, I devised a system using 4-by-6 beams set vertically. I drilled through the beams, then drove a 4-foot pipe through the hole and into the hill, providing good sheer support. Then I strung recycled 2-by-12 lumber between the beams, holding the 2-by-12 in place with sturdy angle irons. This system opened up 100 square feet of new space for me. The vertical arrangement proved ideal for strawberries, herbs, and shallow-rooted leaf plants, such as spinach, chard, and lettuce.

When you set out purposefully to discover your food-growing space, you'll generally find you have more than you anticipated.

The 900 square feet that is sufficient for all our family's vegetables in California's mild year-round climate would have to be 1500 square feet, with plenty of freezer storing space, in Washington, Minnesota, or Maine, which have such short growing seasons.

2: Prepare and Nurture Your Soil

To the dedicated food gardener, soil is something more than just dirt. As an herb is not a weed, a Cabernet is not a vin ordinaire, so good soil is something to appreciate and cherish.

First, determine what you have in soil. Turn a few spadefuls and examine its characteristics with your hand. You'll be able to see one of your soil's three main qualities, its texture. You won't be able to see directly its other two important qualities, nutritive level and pH (its range of acidity/alkalinity).

Chances are your urban soil will be surprisingly good. We humans like to live on our richest farmland, along rivers, around bays, in the lush lowland. The annual loss of farmland to urbanization is a grave long-range problem. You reverse this trend by refarming the city.

As you turn the first spadefuls of soil, feel the texture by rubbing the soil between your fingers. An optimum soil is loose and friable, with plenty of organic material. If your soil particles are extremely small, holding tightly together, you have a clay soil, which will drain slowly and inhibit roots from expanding freely. Water often runs off rather than penetrates clay soil. If water penetrates, it can linger too long at the root level, drowning the plant. However, a clay soil usually contains a considerable reservoir of nutriments.

If your soil is at the other end of the spectrum, with large and loose particles, you have a sandy soil. Sandy soils drain quickly but may have few nutriments. The nitrogen nutriment, especially, can be leached out quickly by rain.

In the middle of the scale are loam soils, with much organic material and moderate-sized particles to give adequate drainage. The texture of all soils can be improved by the addition of organic material.

My soil proved to be a rock and clay mixture. Many hours of strenuous digging were required to remove all the rocks in the areas of my future raised beds. Moistening the soil, but not saturating it, made the digging easier.

The vigor of plant growth will be an index to the reservoir of nutriments and pH range of your soil.

Plants need three main nutriments to grow satisfactorily. The first is nitrogen (atomic symbol N), crucial for vigorous development of the plant's green vegetative growth. The second is phosphorus (P), needed to get good root growth, bloom, set fruit, and resist pests and disease. The third is potassium (K), for strong stems, root development, and disease resistance.

Fertilizers you buy will have numbers on the bags referring to the N, P, and K content. Cottonseed meal will have the numbers 6-4-1. The numbers mean that, by weight, the cottonseed meal is 6 percent nitrogen, 4 percent phosphorus, and 1 percent potassium. Nitrogen is the main nutriment you must resupply to the soil.

Your soil will also need several trace minerals that plants require, such as zinc, iron, and sulphur. The trace minerals are probably already there in adequate supply. If you have a trace mineral deficiency, it will appear in the leaves of your plants. A nurseryman looking at the leaves can usually identify the problem. I add a rock dust trace mineral compound, such as Old Utah Soil, at the rate of 3 pounds per 100 square feet per year to be assured all trace minerals will be present.

Food gardening is a satisfying activity if you proceed by balancing practical experience with your growing theoretical knowledge. When you know something about food gardening from your own experience, you know it absolutely. Peppers will not produce for you or for anyone, anywhere, in the cool season. In the first season, before I understood the matter of N, P, K, I gardened with relative success. My clay soil had a reservoir of nutriments. Eventually I would have depleted them if I had continued without fertilizing. I mention this experience because you need not be paralyzed by seemingly overwhelming technical aspects of food gardening.

The third main consideration in soil is pH. Nutriments may be present, but are they available? Vegetable plants can utilize nutriments best if the soil balance between acidity and alkalinity is about 6.5 on the 0–14 pH scale. Assume you don't have a pH problem unless the plants tell you or unless you have information that your region's soil generally needs some pH correction. Ask an experienced nurseryman about local pH level. Low-rainfall regions tend to have alkaline soils; heavy rainfall areas tend to more acidic soils. Soil pH can be moved from alkaline toward acidic by adding sulphur; soil amendment with dolomite lime alters the pH from acid toward alkaline. Dolomite lime also carries a valued trace mineral, magnesium. Your county extension agricultural agent can assist you with a soil test.

My soil has never had a pH problem. The constant addition of large amounts of organic material serves to buffer any excesses because a well-made compost has an optimum pH.

You can test your soil for pH and for nutriment level with a kit, available at garden stores. Ask for a Sudbury kit or the more precise LaMotte kit. Follow instructions carefully to ensure that your results reveal the actual soil condition.

With this overview in mind, let us consider more thoroughly texture, soil nutriments, and composting.

Improving Texture

There are several good reasons to improve your soil's texture. A soil with good texture holds more water and yet drains well if there is an excess. Roots can travel deep in a soil with good texture, improving the speed of growth for all vegetables and the quality of root vegetables. With an improvement in texture, through the addition of organic material, it is likely your soil will also reach added nutriment levels. Once you have a soil with good texture, never allow it to be compacted with foot traffic.

The classic problem of poor texture has plagued those of us who have clay soils. As a novice, I planted carrots in the clay. The carrot tops widened rapidly until I imagined I would harvest carrots 2 inches wide and a foot long. But when picked, the carrots resembled golf balls. The carrot root was unable to penetrate the clay soil.

Your goal in texture improvement is a simple one: Dig in as much organic material as deeply as possible. You can dig areas efficiently by first taking out all the soil from a trench 1 by 5 feet long and 1 foot deep. That's 5 cubic feet of soil, enough to fill a wheelbarrow and a couple of cardboard boxes. Then fill the hole with organic material. Dig the adjacent area 1 by 5 by 1 foot, putting the soil on top of the organic material. Put more organic material in the second trench. Put the first trench of soil on top of the organic material in the last trench. You will quickly discover the merits of all economy of movement when transferring soil, especially if the day is hot.

With all this talk of organic material, what is it and how do you find it in an urban area? Organic material consists of any matter of plant or animal origin, preferably well composted or rotted. The main sources of organic matter are

your own compost or any composted matter
animal manures (steer and cow, chicken, horse, and rabbit, all better if
relatively litter free and if the animal has had a low salt intake)
leaves and rotted leaf mold
mushroom compost (sold by mushroom companies after they've grown a

crop of mushrooms in it)
sawdust and ground bark (if fresh, add nitrogen to balance its high
carbon content)
peat moss
You can buy organic materials at garden supply stores as "soil amendment." The question is always the amount you need and the price. It may be more cost efficient for you to buy such amendments by the cubic yard if you can strike up a bargain with a nursery or a topsoil company. (Look under "Nursery" or "Topsoil" in the Yellow Pages.) A cubic yard of material goes a long way when you consider the dimensions and break it down. A 3-by-3-by-3-foot cubic yard means 27 cubic feet or 1 inch coverage of 27 by 12 feet, 324 square feet.

Consider first the resources you can get free because they are wastes in your community. Sawdust is a waste at lumber stores, cabinet shops, and furniture factories. Stables have horse manure; dairy farms have cow manure; and chicken ranches have chicken manure.

Each small space vegetable gardener's source for organic material will be different. I'll tell you how I secured mine. When I was building my gardens, the forward-looking city of Berkeley had a program to compost all the city's tree clippings. Huge amounts of organic material that otherwise would have had to fill San Francisco Bay or be trucked off at great expense were shredded, wetted, and processed as compost. You could trade in your tree clippings for finished compost or buy compost at a reasonable price. I secured several cubic yards from this source.

I also made trips into the countryside to get horse manure at local stables. I purchased a dozen burlap bags for 30 cents each from a "Bags, Used" company found in the Yellow Pages. I held the bags in place when loading the manure by slipping them over two finishing nails placed 18 inches apart on a sawhorse. Once a week I put bags, sawhorse, and pitch fork into my VW camper for the manure run. Manure runs were especially useful in the autumn before our seasonal rains. I put in my cabbage family plants, which are heavy nitrogen feeders, and then shored them up with manure, letting the rain soak the nutriments in. With horse manure there were always a few seeds volunteering their presence in the garden, so I followed up to keep the weeds in check. I also bought quantities of mushroom compost from a mushroom company. This compost was made of manure and straw.

Improving the texture of your soil raises the question of tools. Breaking up and moving soil, especially new soil, will strain the best tools. When choosing tools, buy the top of the line, if possible. Or

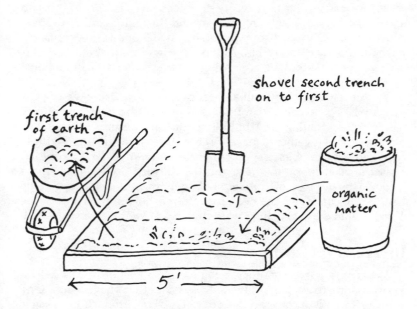

DIGGING IN
ORGANIC MATERIAL

shovel second trench
on to first

first trench
of earth

organic
matter

← 5' →

get used tools of good quality from flea markets, garage sales, and "Tools, Used" businesses found in the Yellow Pages. Poorly made tools prove discouraging in the long run because they break down at exactly the wrong time. The same can be said for garden hoses. Inexpensive plastic hoses without reinforcing will burst in hot weather.

The tools that seem to me most essential for small space vegetable gardening include some unusual ones:

butcher knife	rake
machete	pick
hoe	hammer
pitch fork	hoses and soaker hoses
shovel	Y-valves for hoses
trowel	

All the tools are self-explanatory, except for the first two. A butcher knife is the handiest tool in my garden. I buy a sturdy butcher knife for about $3 at a local hardware store. With the knife I harvest, dig weeds, kill slugs and snails, and perform minor troweling and digging to prepare groundspace for new plants. With the machete I chop up all plant refuse into as fine particles as possible to speed their disintegration into compost. For exercise I chop rather than jog. As a chopping block, I have three railroad ties set on top of each other next to my compost pit. The ties are drilled and a pipe has been sunk into the ground through them. The top tie provides an elevated chopping platform. Chopped materials are pushed into the compost bin. A good machete costs about $7 and is an indispensable tool for processing organic materials in a compost system.

With experience, you will also learn how to devise some of your own tools. For example, I wanted to have all the hose capabilities (spraying, sprinkling, and bubbling) on one hose, so I used two Y-valves fitted together to make three ends for attachments. To these ends I added a bubbler, a sprayer nozzle, and a small lawn sprinkler. I assembled them on the hose and then firmed up the hose with a 4-foot 1-by-1 piece of lumber, held on by plumber's tape. This handy tool cuts down the need for different hoses. A change of the Y-valve allows me to deliver water in any of the three ways desired.

Increasing Nutriments

When the subject of increasing your soil's nutriments arises, know that there are two routes to follow and that I have a bias. One route is the path of conventional commercial fertilizers, the packages of vegetable food 12-10-5 and such at your local garden store. These prepared fertilizers consist of salts formed into pellets or powder that you rake into the soil or use as a side dressing for plants. These conventional commercial fertilizers have some strong attractions at first glance. They are conveniently packaged, compact to transport, and moderately priced (from the consumer's immediate cash perspective). They are usually "complete" in that they have some of each of the three major nutrients, but they sometimes lack important trace minerals.

I don't use these materials, but you may wish to, especially to get started. There are five limitations to this method of fertilizing.

First, these salts (such as ammonium sulfate for nitrogen) add nothing to soil texture. They can be caustic to plants when concentrated, can adversely affect microbial action in the soil, and can change soil chemistry to make it inhospitable to earthworms.

Second, they are usually quick-release fertilizers that wash through the soil and have to be applied repeatedly. After washing through the soil, they accumulate in streams and lakes, disrupting the natural biosystem.

Fertilizers

Type	N-P-K	Activity Span (months)
Basic organic fertilizers		
Compost (my own and purchased)	Variable	
Animal manures (fresh, litter free manures are highest in nutriments)		
Chicken	4.5-6-2.4	
Horse	.7-.3-.6	
Cow or steer	2.5-1.6-3.6	
Rabbit	2.4-1.4-.6	
Mainly nitrogen		
Blood meal (also high in iron)	12.5-1.75-.7	3-4
Fish emulsion (fish products are rich in trace minerals)	5-1-1	6-8
Fish meal	10.5-6-0	6-8
Cottonseed meal	5-2-1	4-6
Hoof and horn	14-2-0	12
Human urine (by dry weight)	46.5-0-0	3
Mainly phorphorus		
Bone meal	3-22-0	6-12
Rock phosphate	0-33-0	36-60
Mainly potassium		
Kelpmeal (many trace minerals)	1-0-12	36-60
Greensand	0-1.5-6.7	36-60
Crushed granite	0-0-5	36-60
Wood ash (use ash from wood but not from inked papers)	0-1.5-7	6
Supplemental fertilizers		
Cocoa bean hulls (good water retainers)	1-1-2	
Trace mineral compound (trade name Old Utah)	Trace minerals	
Sewage sludge (a source with potential, but can be dangerous in some localities because of its possible accumulation of toxic heavy metals, such as cadmium)	6-3-5	

Third, they are extremely expensive for us to produce, as a society, because of the heavy inputs of fossil fuels required in their manufacture. Our current methods of accounting don't project this full cost because depletion is not considered when determining the bottom line. We've decided to let our children and grandchildren pay the depletion price. For a few decades these fertilizers have brought considerable prosperity, but the final cost will be high because the system can't sustain itself as fossil fuels dwindle.

Fourth, salts from these fertilizers can build up in the soil and disrupt fertility. Salts impair the ability of a plant cell to absorb water and nutriments in the process of osmosis.

Fifth, these fertilizers seem to produce plants that are more readily attacked by insects and diseases than the same plants grown with organic methods.

The fertilizers I use and recommend are loosely called "organic" because they generally come from renewable sources, are not harsh on the earth, and require little or no fossil fuel inputs in their creation. These organic soil amendments build soil texture and release their nutriments over long periods of time. They are good fertilizers for a sustainable agriculture. In the table on page 21, they are listed with the main nutriments they supply.

I use some mix of these materials to provide a continuous, gradual feeding program for my soil. Some of the materials are free (my compost, my urine, my fireplace ash). Other materials can be gathered as wastes from the community (animal manures, sawdust). For the priced products, the question is always value for price and often depends on volume bought. In my situation, rock phosphate is a good annual investment.

Urine will probably be considered too much of a taboo for most home gardeners to use. But if you consult your doctor, you will learn that urine is free of any harmful pathogens. Urine is 46.7 percent nitrogen by dry weight. One adult's urine can provide enough nitrogen for about 3000 square feet of garden space. Dilute urine 1:5 with water when applying. Keep your salt intake low if you plan to use your own urine.

Other approaches to nutriment replenishment should also be noted. I plant peas each year because they are delicious and because, as members of the legume family, they have the ability to fix nitrogen from the air into the soil at their root nodes.

Green plants are sometimes grown and then dug under as a "green manure." Clover and rye grass are examples. Other gardeners with larger plots do this, but I don't.

Manures can be used conveniently as a "tea" for plants. I put the manure in a fiberglass bag and steep it in a 5-gallon plastic pail. Then I use a syphon device plugged into the water supply to distribute the tea in a diluted form to the garden. Or I distribute the tea with a ladle to the plants that can use it most readily.

If you feel ambitious about urban self-reliance, you might consider a small chicken or rabbit production system for eggs or meat. The derivative benefit would be a small, constant supply of animal manure for your vegetables.

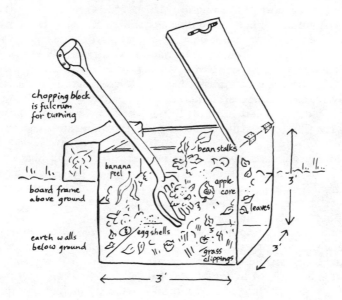

COMPOST   PIT

chop kitchen refuse } to 3/4" pieces
     garden wastes

add leaves
    grass clippings

chopping block
is fulcrum
for turning

board frame
above ground

earth walls
below ground

banana
peel

bean stalks

apple
core

leaves

egg shells

grass
clippings

3'

3'

← 3' →

Composting

Composting, the processing of vegetable and animal remains to recycle them in the garden, is a satisfying, integral part of urban food production. Set up your compost system as soon as possible. Composting permits an elegant, closed cycle in which nutriments are returned to the earth. Imported materials (such as egg shells, orange peels, and coffee grounds) add their nutriment values to the soil through the compost. All vegetative "wastes" suddenly become "resources." Composting even allows you to recycle the concentrated nutriments in the bodies of weeds.

Composting serves many purposes. It allows you to manage wastes, which can be voluminous, especially at seasonal transitions when all the tomato vines or bean stalks are uprooted and removed. When composted, these materials reduce to about 5 percent of their volume. Compost adds immeasurably to soil texture, gradually im-

proving the moisture retention and root expansion possibilities of
your soil. Compost also provides a satisfactory amount of the major
nutriments and minor trace elements at the proper pH for vegetables. Composting prevents soil from eroding due to water and wind
action. The problem with compost will always be that you will have
too little of it.

For the compost processing to work, several conditions must be
met. The volume of material must be of sufficient size, about a cubic
yard. The materials must have a proper carbon-nitrogen ratio
(30:1), which means you must balance any carbon-rich dry materials, such as sawdust, dry leaves, and dry grass, with nitrogen-rich
materials, such as green grass clippings, kitchen scraps, urine, and
animal manures. Chop all materials to ¾-inch size or smaller. The
pile should be wetted thoroughly but not saturated. Periodically,
every few days, materials should be turned to allow more oxygen to
enter.

If all these conditions are working, the compost will heat up to
160° F. and kill weed seeds or any fly eggs in the batch. If you
become skilled at making hot compost, you can add chopped bones,
such as chicken bones, to make your own bone meal, a valued
phosphorus nutriment.

Sometimes a compost system doesn't work well because the
gardener hasn't understood its requirements. Compost making is an
art, requiring an appreciation of balances. If your compost isn't
working, here's how to troubleshoot it. Not heating up? May need
more nitrogen (manure, blood meal, urine). May be too dry (spray
with fine mist). May be too wet (add sawdust and turn often). May
not have enough air (turn more often). Smells of ammonia? Too
much nitrogen, so add sawdust and turn. Smells of swamp gas? Too
much water, resulting in anaerobic (no air) rather than aerobic (air)
decomposition. Turn and add more dry materials, such as sawdust
or leaves.

The ideal composting situation allows you to collect all the materials going into it and then start the compost at one time, processing it hot for about three weeks. However, you needn't be that
rigorous. I find it difficult to adhere to such a plan. I add to my
compost daily with kitchen refuse and vegetative material from the
garden, as the garden generates it. I chop and turn some of my
compost every day.

Every month or so I take out this partially composted material and
put it in an adjacent, smaller compost bin, which I call the "worm
box" because I have a vigorous strain of red worms there to chew up
the compost.

When the compost has been processed in the worm box, I take it out and sift it through a ¼-inch screen mesh, called "hardware cloth." The screen is mounted on a frame. I throw whatever doesn't go through the screen back into the hot compost so it can travel through the system again. I then distribute the sifted compost through the garden, along with any worms riding along. Worms are a valuable asset in the garden, pulling surface organic material deep into the soil and adding air and water passageways with their tunnels.

When planning your compost system, think in terms of your entire setup for processing vegetables. First, you will want to wash the vegetables out in the garden rather than in the kitchen. This will allow you to wash valuable soil off the vegetables and return it to the garden. Aphids, caterpillars, and other wildlife can be removed out of doors rather than in the kitchen. I have a sink and a water supply hooked up in my garden. Washing the vegetables in the outdoor sink allows me to recycle the water to my raised beds. Water conservation with such techniques is a contributing rationale for the philosophy of urban food gardening. Urban water is expensive, costing me about 1 cent per 10 gallons.

Consider building a permanent wooden tool box in the vegetable-processing area to hold your knife, scissors, machete, pruning shears, trowel, twine, hammer, and nails. I use the top of my wooden tool box as a waist-level work platform for cutting up vegetables.

Next, locate the compost pit close to the washing area so you can throw the unused parts of vegetables into it. Plan for a chopping block, such as the three railroad ties mentioned earlier. The three ties also serve as a fulcrum when I use a pitch fork to turn the materials.

I have located my cubic-yard compost pit as a 2-foot-deep pit in the earth. The top foot extends out of the earth and is surrounded by boards. Adjacent is the previously mentioned worm box, constructed similarly, but smaller. Some urban garden enthusiasts make three wooden compost bins on a concrete floor. This idea has some merit. You don't lose any juices in the earth. However, since my pits are adjacent to my avocado tree, I don't mind the losses. Three bins would allow one bin for sorting material before processing, another bin for hot processing, and a third for sorting the processed compost before dispersal. This is a system worth considering, but I prefer my simpler system as more in keeping with the rhythms of my garden and life. When the compost pile is located in the earth, there can also be a free migration of beneficial earthworms in and out.

Take some time to plan your whole vegetable and compost processing system. Make it attractive in appearance and sanitary. Cover the top of the compost pile to keep in the heat and control wetness in

PROCESSING YOUR VEGETABLES

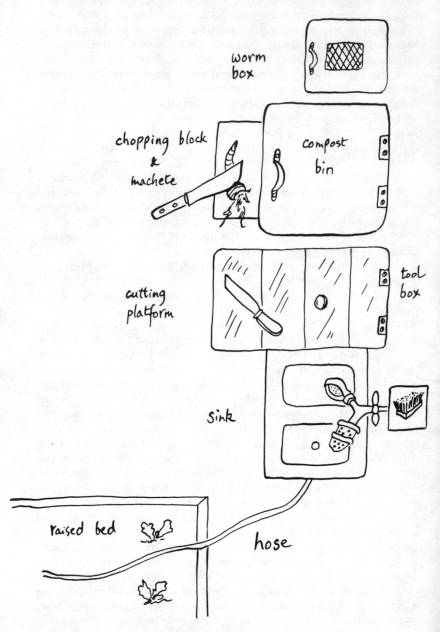

the rainy season. Screen any air openings to reduce fly breeding. You may want to locate your compost system in a shady area that you can't use as a prime growing space.

Composting is possible, but more difficult, in an apartment. You can use a large garbage can, but you will have to give more careful attention to the system. The materials must be chopped finely. Moisture content must be monitored frequently to prevent noxious but harmless odors from anaerobic decay. A fine mesh fiberglass screen, to allow oxygen but deter flies, should be fitted over the top of such a small compost system.

The Romance of Soil

The gradual improvement of your soil over a period of years is exciting to watch. You have created and nurtured the soil. It has given back food to you. The bond grows stronger with each passing season. Everything you put into your soil will come back to you.

Your own food garden can be a satisfying antidote to the environmental deterioration all around you. You are enhancing your soil rather than watching as agricultural soil is exploited and depleted. Your own soil can be a model to provoke larger changes. The survival and flourishing of human culture depends on the fertility of the fragile top 6 inches of the world's topsoil.

Signs of vitality in your soil will be dramatic moments. The first appearance of earthworms, a sign of soil life, will bring joy to you. The improved texture, which can be felt as you squeeze soil between your fingers, will reward you.

From this soil you can produce the food needed to sustain and then enhance life. You can achieve the power to do this. You can manage to live with much less environmental destruction than your previous habits of importing commercial vegetables and fruits has caused. When you grasp your own power in food production, other directions toward a more energy-efficient life-style may also appear.

There is no escaping that food gardening in an ambitious way may take some initial investment. Your cost may be nothing more than a few dollars for seeds. But tools, hoses, and wood for raised beds may run into hundreds of dollars for a complete system. Your time commitment may run into hundreds of hours. But don't approach food gardening with a stopwatch. Food production can be a re-creation, a whole new exuberance in your life. The return on investment in fresh vegetables and herbs will soon pay off. You'll also spend less time waiting in line at a supermarket checkout counter and driving to and from the market in your car, at 20 cents per mile.

3: Effective Planting Techniques

Planting is one of the satisfying moments in food gardening. At the planting, the pattern that will later bring harvest is set. Space is committed. Put some thought into planting before the actual time arises. Consider the layout of your garden. A graph paper can help. How should you allot your space? What vegetables do you and your family like? How long will each vegetable take to mature? What will follow it in the space? What experiments should you undertake this season? How can you extend your growing season at both ends, spring and autumn? This chapter and the next help you answer such questions.

Starting with Nursery Plants

If you are a beginning gardener, you may want to start with nursery plants. Especially in the first season, beginning with an instant garden can boost morale and give you quicker satisfaction, which can increase motivation. Over the long run buying nursery plants for a few varieties has some advantages in small gardens. If you need only a couple of tomato plants and are happy with the variety offered at your local nursery, buying tomato seedlings each year may be the best procedure.

When planting seedlings, either nursery stock or my own seed-raised seedlings, I always wet the ground thoroughly. Then I water heavily the immediate depression into which the seedling will go. I transplant, when possible, in the evening to give the plants the night to recover from the shock. If the plants look droopy the next day, I protect them from the sun with a clay pot or board. The amount of shock a seedling suffers from transplanting depends on the quantity of soil carried on its roots to the new planting area. Ideally, they won't even know they've been transplanted.

Buying nursery seedlings has many disadvantages in the long run and for larger gardens. Root plants, such as carrots and beets, can't be bought in this way because roots are damaged in transplanting. The high cost of nursery plants for many vegetables, such as lettuce, makes starting with seed far more economical. The variety of each vegetable available in seed will also be greater than the variety of seedlings offered. When buying nursery plants, you also relinquish control over the developing seedling, regarding how it was fertilized and watered and what pesticides were used. Eventually, you will probably want to use seeds.

Starting with Seeds

I suggest starting carrots, beets, radishes, and potatoes with seed right in the ground, where they can grow and be harvested. Transplanting these crops can deform the root or tuber.

I grow other vegetable crops in a seed box first, then transplant them into the garden. This strategy is crucial in my desire to use space as effectively as possible. When I take out a pepper plant about October 1, I want to have a broccoli plant 6 inches high ready to occupy the space. Planting a broccoli seed would waste the space for another month and make it unlikely that the broccoli would develop sufficiently before the slow-growing cool winter temperature in my climate.

To start with seeds, you need good potting soil and a secure, sunny place to put the pots or flats. For potting soil you can use your best garden soil, sifted through a ¼-inch mesh screen. If you find the soil has "damping off" fungus that kills seedlings, you can sterilize it in a water-filled pan on an outdoor barbecue for one hour. The temperature should be 180° F. The cooking soil may have a pungent aroma.

I buy a 2-cubic-foot bag of potting soil each year and continue to reuse it for my seedlings. Potting soil is rich in organic material and includes some sand for fast drainage. Commercial potting soil has been steam sterilized to eliminate the damping off fungus and kill weed seeds.

Before planting seeds in this potting soil, I saturate it by placing the soil in a 5-gallon plastic bucket and filling the bucket with water. Once this soil is wetted thoroughly, it holds enough moisture for the seedlings to develop for the first week to ten days.

After a week or so, even my saturated soil will need some additional water. Watering sprouted seeds and seedlings is a delicate operation. I use a small watering can sold for indoor houseplants. The can has a long spout for delicate delivery of water. Water alongside the seedlings, being careful not to knock them down. I leave an inch of space at the top of the pots so I can direct the flow of water against the pot and allow water to run across the surface of the soil. An inch of water in the pots will soak clear through to the bottom.

SEEDLING BOX

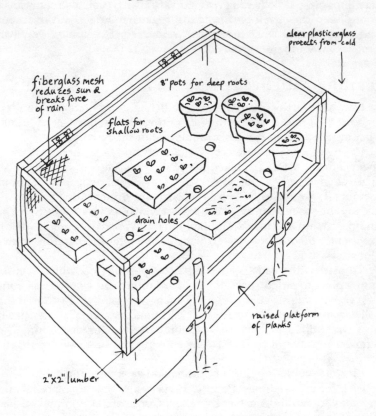

clear plastic or glass
protects from cold

fiberglass mesh
reduces sun &
breaks force
of rain

8" pots for deep roots

flats for
shallow roots

drain holes

raised platform
of planks

2"x2" lumber

I start all my large plant seedlings in 6–8-inch pots, but I sow lettuce, spinach, and onions in flats. In an 8-inch pot I will grow four cauliflower or broccoli plants to 6 inches high, then transplant them to the garden. Squash and cucumber plants are an exception to the strategy of planting roughly four seedlings to an 8-inch pot. Because of their large leaves, they should each have their own pot. Clay pots are preferable to plastic because the clay is porous and can "breathe."

Keep seedlings in a secure box rather than exposed during the germination and initial period of their lives. I have constructed a seed box on a platform of planks, using 2-by-2 framing lumber and fiberglass mesh wire. In periods of intense rain, the fine mesh screen on the top breaks the power of the falling water, which can wash out seedlings. In the cool season I staple plastic sheets over the wire and frame to keep in the sun-generated warmth. The seed box protects young seedlings from the destruction caused by birds, slugs, and snails. Spare yourself the sight of a long row of young seedlings chewed apart because you were unable to maintain proper defenses. Birds are especially fond of tender seedlings in the cool season, when there may be little else in tender green vegetation to eat. When the sugar level of a seedling goes down, as the plant matures, birds cease to attack.

Your own seed box can be as simple as a sunny windowsill in the kitchen or a greenhouse window installed in your house.

Choosing Vegetables

The decision about what vegetables to plant involves many choices. Begin by assessing what vegetables you and your family like to eat. If you like carrots and cauliflower, concentrate on those. If you've never heard of kohlrabi, don't plant it at the start but consider it as an experiment in a future season.

Consider also which favorite vegetables are available in your markets in limited quantities, at high prices, and perhaps in poor condition. Edible pod sugar peas or Sugar Snap peas may be such vegetables.

Note which vegetables are available in your market only in tough shippable varieties. As a home gardener you can improve on commercial lettuce and tomatoes.

Plan for the total time and space in your garden that will be committed to each vegetable. Radishes can be planted 2 inches on centers and harvested in twenty-five days, but leeks, 3 inches on centers, will take one hundred fifty days.

Become aware of the limits of your climate, which may preclude growing certain vegetables. You can modify your climate with cold-frames that increase heat or with lattice coverings that decrease sun intensity, but these alterations are not complete and may require constant attention. You're usually better off, especially when beginning, with vegetables that grow well in your region. I simply don't have the intense heat required for eggplants and melons, so I've learned not to plant them. Heat, fog, cloud cover, humidity, wind, elevation, and the directional orientation of your property are all factors. Begin by consulting a local nurseryman, vegetable gardener, or county extension agricultural agent with experience in your area.

Allow for the important fact that some vegetables grow only in the hot season and others prefer a cool season. Hot season plants benefit from all the sun and warmth they can get. Your hot season

will be the summer months, as mine is, but your cool season may be
a relatively short period before and after or virtually all the rest of
the year, as mine is. The main hot season plants include
   beans
   eggplant
   melons
   peppers
   squash
   sweet corn
   tomatoes
Cool season plants are
   cabbage family
   carrots, beets, radishes
   lettuce
   onion family
   peas
   spinach and other greens
Consider also the anticipated yield from a given vegetable plant.
One or two zucchini plants will supply all you can eat. If you plant
five zucchini, you will probably conclude later that you could have
used the space more wisely. Zucchini doesn't store easily.

Do you have a means to store your surplus crop from the warm
season? I steam beans or chard for five minutes and then freeze them
in bags for use in winter, when I can't grow the plants. Beans are a
good example of a surplus bearing warm weather crop. Most vegetables need to be steamed to kill enzymes that would cause
deterioration of taste and texture even when frozen. Chopped peppers and quartered tomatoes are two exceptions, however. They
don't need to be steamed before being packed in thick freezer bags
and frozen. In the cool season your production will probably not
exceed your consumption, unless you have a very large garden.

Your soil conditions can dictate which of the root crop varieties
you'll choose. I use Chantenay carrots, a thick stubby variety, when
planting in a clay soil that hasn't been loosened thoroughly by
digging in organic material.

With all these considerations in mind, it's time to purchase your
seeds. Make these purchases in your first season at a local nursery,
which will carry seeds proven in your region. Hopefully, your
selection will be guided by knowledgeable personnel. For your second and subsequent seasons of vegetable gardening, write away for
some free seed catalogs of seed companies, listed in Chapter 8. The
seed catalogs will present more options for each vegetable than your
local supplier could offer. However, the varieties may not work as
well in your climate.

Seed catalogs are a wonderful world unto themselves, with lush color photos of vegetables. The photos and reassuring prose can sustain a gardener sitting before the fireplace while the snow flies in February. It is stressful to read seed catalogs on an empty stomach. They present an ideal world untouched by the aphid or the caterpillar.

Once your garden is established, you'll find much pleasure in experimenting with different varieties of the same vegetable. Part of the pleasure of planting your own food garden is that the experience is dynamic, always changing, with the prospect of new types of plants always before you. For example, this past season I concentrated on several hot peppers, Jalapeno, Cayenne, and Pasilla. These peppers were a fresh new taste experience for my family.

Timing Spring Planting

The busiest planting time for most vegetable gardens is in the spring. The juices are flowing and the urge to get going is strong. Your local climate history is the only guide to tell you when to plant. In my almost frost free city of Oakland, near San Francisco, I can grow 365 days a year. If I lived in Bismarck, North Dakota, I would be boxed in by frosts for a short 130-day growing season between mid May and late September.

Arrange to have seedlings ready at the appropriate planting date. Root crops, tubers, and cool season seedlings can be planted at your last approximate frost date. Start the seedlings four weeks earlier. Hot weather plants should be planted two weeks later than your last spring frost date, so start their seedlings a week or two later than the cool season seedlings. As a broad rule, plant your cool weather seeds by April 1, your warm weather seeds by April 15.

The climate at your own property may differ sharply from the general climate in your region. For example, my property is located on a hillside facing south, blessed with a constant solar gain, all year. My gardens are sheltered in a shallow ravine, protected from high winds and frost. The house immediately above mine has a large white wall that bounces sunlight and heat into my backyard garden. An avocado tree flourishes in my backyard because of these special conditions and because my house shields the avocado from wind. Your own climate may have many such eccentricities that you can exploit effectively.

In my climate putting tomato seedlings out in April is a waste of time. They sit there and do nothing. I have to wait until mid June for results. My cabbage family plants must be in by October 1 for good maturation of the broccoli, cauliflower, and cabbage before the

USE SUNLIGHT TO ADVANTAGE

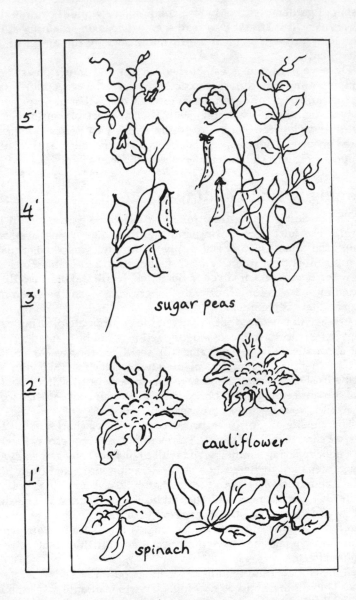

cool season crops

plants go semidormant during the winter. Your own climate will have its limitations. If you plant too early in spring, you can lose the crop to late frosts. Food gardening presents some of the same fascination as other forms of gambling, except that you can rush out on a frosty night and cover your plants with pots or boxes if the roll of the die goes against you.

Positioning Plants

Put the tallest plants in the back and the small plants up front to make good use of sunlight. Plan a stairstep of mature plants. For example, in the cool season, consider putting spinach in the foreground, cauliflower at the intermediate stage, and sugar peas at the back. Visualize in advance what the mature height of the plants will be. With herbs, you must also become aware of height. Dill will grow 4 feet high; basil reaches an intermediate height; and parsley and chive are low plants.

You don't have to plant in rows. After all, you're not planning to drive a tractor through your raised beds, are you? Think in terms of the square inches or feet mature plants need so their leaves are just touching. This leaf canopy in the garden also conserves moisture and reduces weeding. When the sun is low in the sky, increase your spacing slightly. Pathways between raised beds can also be important places for sun entry.

The plants whose fruit we eat (tomato, pepper, squash) benefit from maximum sunlight, but the plants whose leaves we eat (lettuce, spinach, chard, collards, kale) do reasonably well in partial shade. Plant accordingly.

Finally, the length of day and night is a trigger for some plants, telling them to go to seed. In my first year I tried hard to grow spinach by planting it in April. By June the spinach suddenly went to seed. I learned that spinach must be planted either earlier or later to avoid the time of maximum sunlight, which triggers a seeding mechanism.

Watering Effectively

An adequate delivery of water to your vegetables, herbs, and fruits is an essential part of good gardening. When properly watered, plants grow quickly to a lush maturity and have optimum taste and insect resistance. Along with nutriments and air, water is an essential of life for plants. Those of us who garden in the arid West must plan to deliver water from April through October. Gardeners in the

EFFECTIVE WATERING

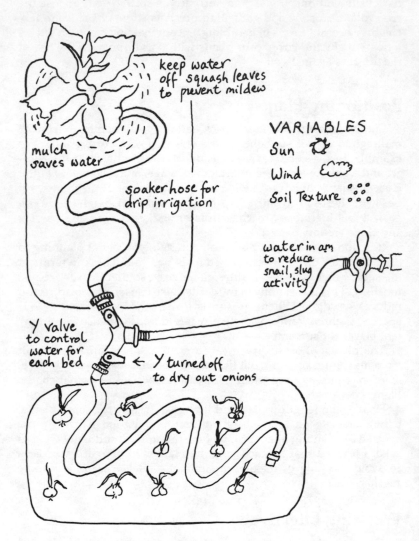

keep water
off squash leaves
to prevent mildew

mulch
saves water

soaker hose for
drip irrigation

VARIABLES
Sun
Wind
Soil Texture

water in am
to reduce
snail, slug
activity

Y valve
to control
water for
each bed

← Y turned off
to dry out onions

Midwest and East can depend on seasonal rains to do much of their watering.

Watering affects both the plant and the gardener. Watering takes time. Standing there with a hand-held hose may be a satisfying meditative activity for some gardeners, but I prefer a system that frees me to harvest, sow, and maintain plants while hoses do the work.

I learned this the hard way. After my first year of intensive gardening, I had all the beds developed but no way except a sprinkler hose to deliver water. I remember how I had to keep moving the hose. On a hot and windy summer day it seemed I was tied to this task for an hour or two.

Now I have soaker hoses in all my beds, hooked up with Y-valves to a central faucet. By changing the valves every twenty minutes on a midsummer day, I can deliver water to all my areas. I have even punched a pipe underneath the sidewalk to install a soaker hose in the median strip, where I raise potatoes and flowers. All the water gets carried through soaker hoses and delivered either on the surface or 6 inches under the ground. The water pressure I choose determines whether the round fiberglass hose soaks or sprinkles. At the height of summer, I must water half my garden one day and the other half the second. With the soaker hoses, I can accomplish this task with five minutes committed over a period of an hour a day.

Watering is an art as well as a science. Pay some attention to your own watering system and it will reward you with consistently high-quality food production at minimal cost.

The two main questions in watering are how much and how often. Your soil will tell you. If your soil is clay, an inch of water on the surface will go down about 6 inches. On loam soil, an inch of water goes down 7 inches. On sandy soil, 12 inches. Water tends to go straight down, not sideways, in the soil. So water as close to directly overhead of the root as possible. Determine how deep the roots of your plants are. Then water thoroughly, but only as frequently as needed, to soak the deepest part of the plant's root. Surface watering is not helpful at all. Only deep watering of roots will promote the plant's growth.

The plant's own demands will tell you. Lettuce has shallow roots in the top inches of soil. So the top must be kept moist, perhaps daily in the hottest and sunniest time of summer. Strawberries also need constant water near the surface for the fruit to develop properly. An established tomato plant can draw up the deep water, but it needs much water if you are going to harvest its fruit. Too much water can drown a plant, causing leaves to turn yellow. Too little will cause a plant to wilt. Garlic and bulb onions should be allowed to dry out as their tops start to die back.

· Air temperature, air humidity, and sun intensity will tell you. Your own experience in the first season of vegetable gardening will indicate that in early spring and later autumn, when the sun is low in the sky, the days are short, and the air temperature is cool, your plants will use less water. However, don't let them dry out just because the air is cool. Wind is also an important factor. In windy weather your plants will need much more water, especially the leafy plants that transpire so much water.

The size of your water reservoir will tell you. You will soon learn that a smaller container must be watered every day in the hot, sunny summer. The same plant established in the ground will need less frequent watering.

Mulches help. The addition of organic mulch material on the top of the soil around plants conserves water, keeps the soil temperature even, and eventually adds some fertilizing value. Cocoa bean hulls are an exotic mulch that absorbs two and a half times its weight in water. Grass clippings, sawdust, pine needles, ground bark, newspapers, and leaves are more common mulches.

Conserving water makes sense. In the West we are on a collision course of expanding water use and a finite rainfall source. Annual rainfall in recent decades has been more generous than tree rings indicate it normally should be.

Save water with drip irrigation, using round soaker hoses, with each bed independent. Join soaker hoses between beds with a regular hose so water isn't lost on pathways. I use flexible copper tubing and clamps. One other drip water technique is to punch a hole in the cap of a gallon wine jug, fill the jug with water, and place it on its side near a thirsty plant.

Pathways can also conserve water by catching any rainwater that falls on your property. Bark chips, wood chips, and sawdust on pathways keep water from running off. Runoff of water in urban areas, where more and more soil is paved over, is an increasing problem. A rain barrel stationed at downspouts to collect water can also assist in water collection. Water can be piped from the barrel through the garden.

Extending Your Growing Season

You can extend your spring growing season by building a cold-frame to start seedlings in or by starting them indoors on a windowsill, in a greenhouse window, or in a full-sized greenhouse. The larger the plants you can put out in the spring, the sooner you can harvest.

In the autumn, extend your season with coverings that trap solar heat on the plants. Movable cloches and transparent plastic hotboxes can be placed in the garden. Wire and plastic wraps can be purchased. You can also make these from scrap wood with plastic sheets stapled on. In autumn be ready with plants such as collards, kale, and others in the cabbage family that can take some light frost and still produce. You can also "store" mature root crops, such as beets and carrots, in the ground.

If you have plants in containers, you might be able to move them indoors or to your sunniest location.

In my mild climate, I am fortunate because many plants, such as the herbs oregano and rosemary, easily winter over.

Tips for Effective Planting

Here are a few more tips to consider for an effective planting strategy:

If you have several places on your property to consider for the vegetable garden, choose the area with best drainage. Rain saturating the soil during the wet season can drown plants if the water table rises too high.

Place your herbs as close to the kitchen as possible. You'll be more inclined to get that pinch of oregano if the walk isn't too far.

Keep all perennial vegetables, such as artichokes and asparagus, in beds that you won't have to dig up.

Put corn on the north side of a bed because it is extremely tall and will shade other vegetables.

Place rambling vine plants, such as squash and cucumbers, on the edge of beds so their leaves and stalks can spill over into pathways or into nongarden spaces rather than into the precious space within the center of the bed.

Determine the length of your growing season from spring frost to autumn frost and then try to choose vegetables to get two crops, if possible, from much of your space. Here are some combinations to consider:

First crop	Second crop
early lettuce	*carrots*
beets	*broccoli*
early corn	*bush beans*
pole beans	*early cabbage*
carrots	*collards, kale*
tomato	*cauliflower*
zucchini	*brussel sprouts*

For best space utilization, keep two strategies working for you: Choose short season varieties that mature quickly and have seedlings ready to plant in any space you vacate.

4: The Principal Vegetables

The average size of a home food garden in the United States is 595 square feet, costing $19 to sow and yielding $387 in produce at market prices. The tomato is the most popular vegetable, followed by onions, green beans, cucumbers, peppers, lettuce, radishes, carrots, peas, and corn. The average adult eats 322 pounds of vegetables and fruits per year, 120 pounds of which are potatoes.

If you plan to join the large fellowship of food gardeners (43 percent of American households), you'll need some basic advice on the principal vegetables to plant, plus some strategy for maximum production in small spaces, and a little information on which vegetables are the most nutritious to plant. When you consider the principal vegetables, the following questions may come up.

How deep should you plant the seed? Plant to three times the diameter of the seed. If your soil is soft and fluffy, seeds will be able to break through from a little deeper.

How long will the seed take to germinate? The time varies with different vegetables. Radishes shoot right out, but carrots can linger for three weeks. Ground should remain moist and air temperature remain in the middle range for good germination.

How many days to transplant size? I transplant all my crops except the root vegetables (beets, carrots, radishes), tubers (potatoes), and onion family grown from sets (garlic, bulb onion). The transplant size is usually reached in about four to five weeks. So if you need to have seedlings ready at a certain time, count backwards on your calendar and plant.

How many days until harvest? This knowledge will be crucial if you want to plant two or more harvests per season. Within each vegetable family, such as corn, there will be varieties that mature more quickly than others. Consider such information, printed on the back of seed packs or clearly stated in catalogs, before purchasing. You might want some early tomatoes and later tomatoes. Harvests can be prolonged for cut-and-come-again greens (chard, collards, kale) by cutting outer leaves and for fruiting plants (beans, peas, cucumbers, summer squash) by continual removal of small fruits.

How much space for each vegetable? I consider what space is

needed for the plant, allowing its outer leaves to touch its neighbor's leaves at maturity. Then I stagger the plants in the garden on centers the appropriate distance apart. I plant constantly in each available space, as it comes free, which also leads to a diversity of crops, slowing insect pests that would thrive in a monoculture.

The amount of space you allow per plant will depend on several variables: fertility of your soil, intensity of your sun, angle of sun at this season, size and variety of vegetable chosen, and whether you desire more small vegetables or a few larger vegetables. As a rule, plant so a canopy of leaves covers the ground. Crowding plants beyond that will produce inferior crops because energy will be devoted to fighting for sunlight.

What yield can you expect per square foot? Tomatoes, summer squash, chard, and pole beans are my big providers. The root crops can also produce handsomely.

In condensed form, the chart on the next page describes some of my experience with the principal vegetables.

Now let us consider the principal vegetables, noting their general qualities, cultivation requirements, pests to guard against, time until harvest, and suggestions for good varieties to start with.

Beans

Green and yellow fresh snap beans are a prolific warm weather crop. When looking at a seed packet, be sure to read whether the variety is a bush or a pole type. Bush beans yield sooner, but in smaller quantities, than pole beans. Pole beans take a little longer to flower and fruit, but once they produce, you can often get several meals ahead in one day from a short row. Beans, a New World addition to our diet, are legumes that help fix nitrogen in the soil.

Beans like a sunny location. Be sure to locate pole beans on the north side of the bed to prevent them from shading other crops. Pole beans are such vigorous climbers that they need little tending in my garden beyond a sturdy twine climbing frame. Keep the plants well watered and don't try to extend their growth beyond the autumn frost date. Beans don't like frost.

Aphids are the only bean pest of consequence in my garden. I hose the aphids off with a fine water spray applied to the underside of the leaves. When the aphids begin to appear, the bean plant is generally ready to be pulled and composted. Encourage ladybug populations to check aphids.

I harvest beans twice a week, removing all beans between 6 and 10 inches. Don't let the beans get larger or the plant will believe it has fulfilled its role, gone to seed, and can cease to produce.

Vegetable	Temperature Required (hot or cool season)	Depth to Plant Seeds (inches)	Days to Germination	Days to Transplant Size (or plant direct)	Days to Harvest	Space to Allow for Mature Plants (inches square)	Yield (pounds per square foot) (time not considered)
Beans	H	1	6–14	25	60–70	6	.8
Bush							
Pole							
Cabbage family	C	½	3–10	35	90–115	18	.7
Cabbage							
Broccoli							
Cauliflower							
Brussel sprouts							
Corn	H	2	6–10	15	60–90	12	.5
Cucumbers	H	1	6–10	28	55–65	18	1.6
Eggplant	H	¼	6–10	42–63	90–130	18	1.0
Leaf crops	C	½	3–10	25	40–65		
Chard						12	2.2
Spinach						6	.6
New Zealand spinach (OK in H)						18	1.8
Kale						18	1.1
Collards						18	1.1
Mustard						10	1.4
Lettuce	C	¼	4–10	21–25	45–80	8	1.4
Leaf							
Head							
Melons	H	1	4–8	21–28	75–100	36	.8
Onion family	C	½ for seed;	7–12		95–140		1.5
Bunch				60		1	
Bulb		1 for		60 or set		4	
Garlic		set,		set		4	
Leeks		clove		60		4	
Peas	C	1	6–15	25	65–85	6	.7
Peppers	H	¼	10–20	42–65	80–100	18	.6
Root crops, tubers	C						
Beets		½	7–10	all	55–65	4	1.2
Carrots		½	15–25	direct	60–80	3	1.3
Radish		½	3–10		20–50	3	1.4
Potato		4	6–16		90–105	12	1.4
Squash	H	1	3–12	25	50–60	48	2.2
Summer (zucchini, yellow)							
Winter & pumpkin					85–120	48	2.0
Tomato	H	½	6–14	28–35	60–120	36	2.2

Plant every couple of weeks during the season to keep a constant supply coming. I eat them by steaming for ten minutes or store them in the freezer after steaming for five minutes to kill enzymes that cause deterioration even when the beans are frozen.

Good varieties: Kentucky Wonder, Provider.

Cabbage Family

The cabbage family heading plants (cabbage, broccoli, cauliflower, and brussel sprouts) are good spring and autumn growers. My garden in October is a sea of cabbage family crops. If you raise these plants in the spring, try to move them along to develop heads before the hot weather sets in, when they can bolt to seed.

Cabbage family plants like cool, moist environments, so don't hesitate to sprinkle the leaves. For broccoli and cauliflower, you are eating the immature flower. Plant your seedlings in time for the transplants to reach maturity before autumn frosts. All cabbage plants can take some light frost, but growth will be slow in frosty temperatures.

Heavy nitrogen is desirable for cabbage family plants. Manure tea can be used to advantage with them. Stake the plants well if your region is windy. I drive 1-by-1 lumber stakes beside each plant when I set them out as seedlings.

Two main pests attack the cabbage family. A white butterfly, called the cabbage moth, lays its eggs on the leaves. The green woolly caterpillars hatch and strip the leaves. Observe when the moths are flying and combat them with Bacillus thuringiensis (trade names Dipel, Biotrol, Thuricide), a natural spore. Mix the powder 1 tablespoon to a gallon of water and spray the plants. The spore disrupts the caterpillar's digestion but has no known harmful effect on other insects, plants, or animals. The cabbage moth becomes less of a problem as cool autumn weather stops its life cycle. During the season the moth flies, I spray my cabbage family plants once a week. The caterpillar must ingest a bit of the leaf for the spore to do its work.

Grey aphids are also a problem with cabbage family crops. They are easy to detect on the broad leaves and can be dislodged with a fine, powerful spray of water. When disrupted, they take time to recover. Also, encourage your local population of ladybugs, which eat aphids, and keep flowering plants available at all times to nurture small wasps, which lay their eggs in aphid eggs.

Harvest cabbage when the heads are full. Broccoli should be cut when the head is firm, before the flowers start to open. After the main head is cut, the plant will send out side sprouts, which can also be harvested. Cauliflower should be harvested when the curds are firm, before they begin to separate. Brussel sprouts should be harvested when the side sprouts at the bottom reach golf ball size.

Good varieties of cabbage: Early Jersey Wakefield (green), Mammoth Red Rock (red). Broccoli: Italian Green Sprouting, Green Comet. Cauliflower: Snowball, Self Blanche. Brussel sprouts: Jade Cross.

Corn

Corn is a luxurious vegetable for the food gardener who has plenty of space. Corn is a New World grass, the basis of the advanced early civilizations of Mexico, Guatemala, Peru, and elsewhere.

Both the taste and nutrition of corn are superlative. The taste of sweet corn and Sugar Snap peas are two gourmet experiences the food gardener can provide for his or her family that the market can never equal. In both these vegetables the sugars at picking time turn rapidly to starches. Some corn pickers insist you should put the pot on to boil before you go into the garden to harvest. Varieties are available with kernels that are white, gold, or white and gold mixed.

The pollination of corn is unusual. Bees or other insects pollinate most vegetables, but wind pollinates corn. Consequently, plant four or more rows of corn to get good pollination. Sixteen would be the minimum number of plants (a four-by-four block). Corn likes hot weather, maximum sunlight, and plenty of nitrogen.

The corn ear worm is the only significant pest. If you detect a worm problem, cut the silk off after pollination to prevent the fly from laying its eggs on them. The larvae subsequently crawl up the silk and into the ear.

Plant a succession of corn to have a steady supply or choose varieties that mature early, middle, and late. Harvest when the silk is dry and the ears are plump. When you break a ripe kernel, a milky substance exudes. Pick all corn at its peak because it won't improve with further aging.

Good varieties: Silver Queen, Illini Extra Sweet.

Cucumber

The cucumber so prized now in our salads is thought to have been cultivated first in India.

Cucumbers like a well-composted soil with plenty of heat, but they also like some shade. To minimize the possibility of bitterness and thick skins in cucumbers, grow the plant quickly with plenty of water and nutriments.

Cucumber beetles are sometimes a pest, but they can be hand

Garden Record Keeping

MY VEGETABLE GARDEN	Beans	Brocc
DO I LIKE IT?	Yes	
COOL/HOT SEASON?	Hot	
SUN REQUIREMENTS?	Maximum	
TIME TO MATURE?	60 days	
SPACE/YIELD?	1 lb. per foot	
RECOMMENDED VARIETIES?	Kentucky Wonder	
SEED OR SEEDLINGS?	Either	
MAIN PESTS?	Aphids	
CULTIVATION PRACTICES?	Heavy nitrogen feeder	
WHEN TO HARVEST?	6-9 inches	

picked. Wilt-resistant varieties minimize the prospect of loss due to disease.

Harvest when the cukes are 8 inches to encourage the plant to produce more. Some varieties require harvesting when less than 8 inches.

Good varieties: Saladin, Sweet Slice.

Eggplant

Eggplant should be considered if you have plenty of heat and strong sunlight. Put the seedlings in early for best results, but don't let the plants get chilled.

The range of eggplant varieties available in seed greatly exceeds those in the market. You can raise white as well as purple eggplants of different sizes.

Eggplants like a soil with plenty of organic materials. Keep the plants well watered. Eggplants are strong nitrogen feeders, so supply them constantly with a manure tea while they're growing.

If aphids attack your eggplants, hose them off. Hand pick any Colorado beetles that appear.

Harvest when the eggplant has reached a plump size and the skin is still glossy. The eggplant is ready when the skin breaks easily if pressed with a fingernail. Eggplants are delicious when simmered in tomatoes, garlic, and peppers.

Good varieties: Black Beauty, Black Magic.

Leaf Crops

Vegetables whose green leaves we eat are among our most nutritious foods.

Chard, which was enjoyed by the Romans, is actually a beet whose leaves are edible.

Spinach has leaves so tender I often eat them raw in salad.

Kale and collards are members of the cabbage family whose leaves we eat. They are extremely nutritious.

Mustard is another tasty green.

All the leaf plants do well in cool weather. New Zealand spinach and collards withstand hot weather without bolting to seed.

Leaf crops like a well-composted soil with plenty of nitrogen. They grow well in sun or partial shade.

Spinach has a strong built-in trigger to go to seed as the daylight grows longer. I harvest the entire plant at maturity, though some gardeners make repeated harvests of outer leaves. Plant as early as possible to harvest before the long days of the latter half of June, or else plant spinach for the autumn.

Aphids attack kale, collards, and aging chard. Hose the aphids off with a fine, strong spray of water.

Aside from spinach, harvest these plants by cutting the outer leaves. Cut-and-come-again plants will produce abundantly.

Good varieties: Chard: Rhubarb, Fordhook Giant. Spinach: Melody, All America. Kale: Curley Scotch, Hanover. Collards: Georgia, Vates. For New Zealand spinach and mustard, just ask for them by name.

Lettuce

Fresh lettuce is a garden treat, especially since you can grow succulent varieties that can't be shipped to markets without bruising. I usually concentrate on leaf lettuce, whose leaves can be clipped repeatedly, as needed.

Cultivation for lettuce requires plenty of water, applied frequently, because the roots are shallow. Lettuce will wilt or go to seed in extremely hot weather, so protect it with some shade. Lettuce grows reasonably well in partial shade throughout the cool season and in soils with modest nutriments.

Slugs and snails are the main attackers of lettuce. Control by hand picking and with barriers of sawdust between beds.

Harvest the leaves as needed or take out the whole plant.

Good varieties: Oak Leaf, Black Seeded Simpson.

Melons

If you have both the heat and the space, the sweet taste of vine-ripened melons can be yours. In mild climates, try growing melons in a coldframe.

Bush varieties have been developed to cut down somewhat on space. Smaller melons can also be trained vertically on lathe racks, but be sure to give the developing melon a strong sling as a support.

Melons benefit from maximum sunlight and from plenty of water, but the soil should be well drained. Since a melon is mainly water, it's little surprise that the plant requires much moisture. Melons thrive in soils rich in organic material.

When you water, bubble onto the ground rather than sprinkle the leaves. Wet melon leaves will develop mildew. Striped beetles sometimes attack melons but can be controlled with hand picking.

Pick melons when the stems are dry, the fruit smell is sweet, and the end opposite the stem is slightly soft.

Good varieties: Minnesota Midget (cantaloupe), Golden Midget (watermelon).

Onion Family

It is difficult to imagine a dinner at my house without at least one member of the onion family making a contribution. Garlic, fresh basil leaves, and oil mixed in the blender as a pesto sauce or leeks cut up in a split pea soup provide fond culinary moments here.

Onions are long-term space investments in the garden. Bunch onions are available within 90 days for salads and stir fry cooking, but leeks may occupy the ground for 150 to 160 days.

Onion family members like cool weather. They tend to grow green stems in cool weather and develop bulbs in warm weather, though length of day also triggers the bulbing mechanism. October is the garlic and bulb onion planting month in my mild winter climate. You may need to plant at the earliest date in spring.

Onions like plenty of organic material, but not raw manure, and must be kept moist during the growing season. For garlic and bulb onions, withdraw the moisture in the last month of their growth as the bulb forms. Onion family plants grow well in full sun or partial shade. Grow leeks for their thick edible stems. Mound the soil around the leek plant to lengthen the tender stem. I sometimes plant bunch onions and leeks in clumps rather than in carefully spaced patterns.

Aphids sometimes attack onion family plants, including garlic, regardless of what all the books tell you. Blasts of fine sprays of water can dislodge aphids easily from onion family stems. Fly larvae sometimes attack the roots of onions. Keep rotating the onions in your soil.

Harvest bunch onions when they are pencil thick or thicker, as you need them. Bulb onions should be harvested after the stems have dried back. Knock down the last few stems, let the onions dry out for two weeks, then harvest and let them sun cure for another two weeks. Be careful not to bruise the onions. Garlic is excellent green, cut up like bunch onions. To get the garlic head, let the top die back and harvest as you would bulb onions. Leeks are ready when the thick stems are an inch wide. The whole leek plant is edible, but the white stem is the more succulent part. The green tops are excellent sauteed.

Good varieties: Bunch onions: White Bunching. Bulb onions: Sweet Spanish, Torpedo. Leeks: American Flag. Garlic: Red, White.

Peas

Edible pod sugar peas are a gastronomic delight that the home gardener can create but the market can never equal. That's because the sugar in peas, as in corn, turns to starch quickly after picking.

The traditional sugar pea of Chinese cooking has been joined by the new Sugar Snap pea, which has thicker pods, greater production, heavier weight, and sweeter taste. Peas are not only delicious, they are high in protein and vitamins.

Peas like cool, moist climates. They burn out in the high heat of summer. Like the other common legume, beans, peas fix nitrogen in the soil along their root nodes. Peas are poor climbers, so be ready with constant twine resupporting as the stalks grow. Unsupported stalks are quickly broken off in the wind. Weed carefully so you don't disrupt the shallow roots.

Aphids are sometimes a pest on peas. Hose off the aphids and encourage predacious ladybugs and wasps. As pea vines mature, keep water off the leaves because they will eventually mildew and rot.

Harvest peas when they are 6 inches long. I harvest twice a week. Paradoxically, Sugar Snap peas seem to get sweeter as they mature, so wait until the pods have swollen, if you can. Keep pea vines picked to stimulate more production. Use two hands when picking because the vines are tender and can easily be torn.

Good varieties: Sugar Snap, Mammoth Melting Pod.

Peppers

Peppers are an excellent vegetable to grow for their fresh crisp taste and high nutritive levels. I particularly like to experiment with hot peppers. A few hot pepper plants can produce enough to last our family all year round. In the autumn I dice extra peppers and then freeze them in small individual bags. Peppers and tomatoes don't need steaming before freezing. Peppers can also be dried on your oven rack or in a drier.

Peppers like the hottest weather and sunniest location they can get. Water thoroughly, but make sure the soil drains well. Peppers thrive in rich organic soil with plenty of nutriments. Peppers are a good border or container plant.

I have never had a pest or disease problem with peppers.

Harvest as the peppers reach full size and assume a glossy surface texture. If your climate is dry, you can also let peppers dry on the vine. However, I prefer to pick at their peak and then freeze the excess.

Good varieties: Sweet Pepper: Yolo Wonder. Hot Pepper: Jalapeno.

Root Crops and Tubers

Root crops and tubers are heavy producers. Among the root crops, radishes are the fastest grower in the garden, some varieties coming to maturity in just twenty-five to thirty days. Such radishes are excellent catch crops to put between seedlings, such as tomatoes or cabbage family. Harvest the radish just as the canopy of developing leaf from the seedlings is about to shield it from the sun. Root crops like cool weather best. They will be tougher and less tasty in the hot season. Some radishes become hot as glowing coals at the height of midsummer heat.

Root crops like full sun but will also grow well in some shade. Keep all the root crops well watered. If roots dry out, they can crack. Keep weeds down because root crops lie so close to the ground that they can't bear the competition. Soil must be soft and deep for best root crop development. Plant successively for a continuous harvest. Unlike most vegetables, all the root crops and tubers should be planted directly into the ground. Their roots, the edible part, are disfigured by transplanting. Make sure that potatoes are planted deep enough, about 4 inches, with the seed potato cut into 3 or more pieces, each with an eye or two. Continue to mulch or hill up the potato as the green top develops. Potatoes like a slightly acid soil, so hold the lime and add a little sulphur if a soil test shows your pH to be neutral.

Birds can be serious pests to the tender seedlings of root crops, so watch the birds as the seedlings develop. I protect root seedlings from birds with chicken wire frames that can be moved around the garden to the area needing protection. Larvae of various flies attack root crops. Spread wood ash to deter these flies. The Colorado potato bug may attack potatoes but can be controlled by hand picking.

Harvest beets starting with the thinnings. Beet leaves are tasty and nutritious. Small beets at 1 inch are a delicacy; fully grown beets may reach 4 inches. In summer, harvest carrots when they have reached the optimum size for the particular variety. Don't wait or the carrots can grow woody and burst. In autumn and winter carrots can be stored in the ground. Spring carrots can be thinned and eaten as baby carrots, but production is highest from full-grown carrots. Test occasionally by pulling samples. New potatoes in June are a delicacy. Harvest when the flowers appear. Late potatoes give a greater yield. Harvest when the plant tops die back.

Good varieties: Beets: Detroit Dark Red, Early Wonder. Carrots: Chantenay, Danvers Half Long. Radishes: Crimson Giant, French Breakfast. Potatoes: Red Lasado, White Rose.

Squash

Summer zucchini squash is one of the most prolific plants in my garden. Two plants are sufficient to supply my family throughout

the summer season. Mostly I eat squash lightly steamed or sometimes even raw if quite small.

Though squash vines have a reputation as big space grabbers, you
can now get many squash in bush varieties.

Squash require a hot season, plenty of sun, and a constant supply
of water. Squash like a soil rich in organic material and full of the
major nutriments.

Striped cucumber beetles attack some squash vines. If you detect
them, pick them off. Water the ground rather than the leaves of
mature plants to keep down mildew.

Harvest the summer squash when the immature fruits are 10
inches long. Bigger is not better with zucchini. Harvest also to keep
the plant producing. If you allow a zucchini to get large, the plant
gets a signal that its work is done, that it has fulfilled its role to
produce seed that will carry on the life force. Harvest winter squash
in October when the vines have died back and the skins are thick. To
prevent rotting, be sure to leave on the last 2 inches of vine when
removing the squash. Winter squash can be stored at 55° F. for
several months. Pumpkin seeds can be roasted and shelled. Triple
Treat is a pumpkin with an edible seed that has no hull.

Good varieties: Summer squash: Zucchini, Yellow Crookneck.
Winter squash: Acorn, Butternut. Pumpkin: Big Max, Triple Treat.

Tomatoes

Tomatoes are the favorite vegetable of home gardeners, and for
good reason. They're tastier than the bounceable rubber squares
available in the market. They're productive, with my 4-by-4-foot
space allotment for circular tomato cage and sun space producing
about 35 pounds of fruit. They're also beautiful to look at, hanging
on the vines, ripening slowly to deep red. We have Peru to thank for
the tomato.

Tomatoes like plenty of heat, all the sunlight you can give them, a
steady supply of water, and a rich soil full of organic material and
nutriments. Set out the seedlings with the stalk buried to the lowest
leaves of the plant. I suggest driving a 2-by-4 stake about 6 inches
from the seedling at planting and then fashioning a 6-foot-high wire
cage out of concrete reinforcing wire. The wire has handy 6-inch
squares for reaching in to pick the fruit. Shape the wire into a cage
with a 3-foot diameter. Then drive a nail into the center of the 2-by-4
and tie with twine to the cage in all four directions. A 2-by-4 may
seem like a sturdier piece of lumber than you'll need, but few sights
are more disappointing than a tall tomato plant with 25 pounds of
immature fruit on it blown over by wind, tearing out the root. As the

TOMATOES

Big Boy

Sweet 100

tomato plant grows, keep pushing back into the cage the branches that protrude. The cage gives good air circulation, minimizing the buildup of mildew and rot disease. The cage also keeps all fruit off the ground, which is crucial because tomatoes on the ground rot quickly or are attacked by pests, such as slugs. The cage supports an umbrella of foliage that protects the fruit from sunburn.

The setting of fruit for tomatoes can be tricky. Start with a variety known to produce well in your climate. I suggest buying your first plants or seeds from a local nursery before expanding into exotics you might find in seed catalogs. For the fruit of most tomatoes to set, the nighttime temperature should be around 60° F. If fruit is not setting, strike the plant at midday to disturb pollen and cause fertilization. Tomato fruits set best in soil rich in phosphorus and a pH at 6.8–7.

Tomatoes rarely suffer from pest damage. The large tomato hornworm is a frightening creature to meet for the first time. The hornworm is the caterpillar of the hawk moth and can strip leaves at an alarming rate. If you see damage, track down the hornworm and destroy it. They camouflage well, but their large size and trail of black droppings give them away. If many hornworms occur, spray plants with the biological spore, Bacillus thuringiensis (trade name Dipel, Biotrol, Thuricide), which disrupts the digestion of caterpillars and causes death. If you suffer a wilt problem with your tomatoes, rotate the plants and choose a variety that has wilt resistance, which will be indicated by "V" and "F" on the label.

Harvest tomatoes when they are red ripe. The period lasts for several days, so the day of harvesting is not critical. Vine-ripened tomatoes have a superior taste. When the weather cools and tomatoes will no longer ripen, bring them inside, wrap them individually in newspaper, and set them in a cool place on a screen. The newspaper will keep in gas that stimulates ripening. An apple placed amid tomatoes will give off a gas that hastens ripening. For a good supply of tomatoes all through the season, choose different varieties that have early, middle, and late maturing dates. I store my surplus red tomatoes in summer by slicing them into quarters or into eighths for large Beefsteak types and then freezing them in plastic bags for winter cooking use.

Good varieties: Sweet 100 (Cherry), Big Boy.

Maximum Production

In my small space garden, I always try to plan for maximum production. Here are my recommendations for a 5-by-10 foot bed.

Plant the north side with pole beans (Kentucky Wonder) climbing

MAXIMUM PRODUCTION
IN
MINIMUM SPACE

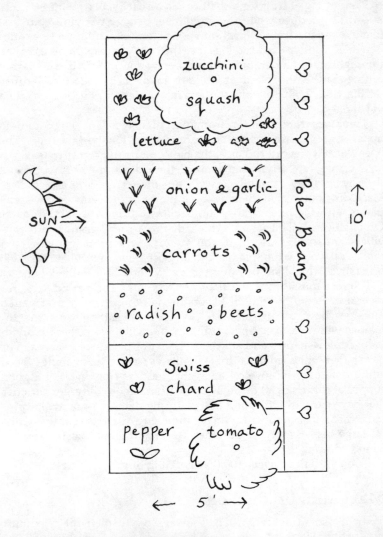

Hot Season Crops

NUTRITIOUS VEGETABLES

(Numbers refer to Recommended Daily Allowance vitamins/
minerals present at levels of 10% or more per serving.)

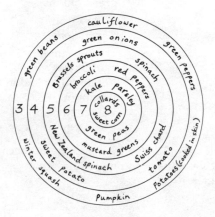

on a rack. If there is a cool season before or after, plant peas (Sugar Snap). On one end put a tomato plant (Sweet 100) with a green pepper (Yolo Wonder). At the other end, 1 foot in, put a zucchini (Black Zucchini), directing the leaves to grow beyond the bed. A good crop of leaf lettuce (Black Seeded Simpson) is possible in the early part of the season where the leaves of the zucchini will eventually spread into the bed. Divide the rest of the bed into 2-by-4-foot plots and plant one with chard (Lucullus), another with onion and garlic, and the third with beets (Detroit Dark Red), radishes (Crimson Giant), and carrots (Chantenay). The chard can be harvested continually as leaves develop.

High Nutrition

When choosing vegetables for your garden, consider crops that have a large range of vitamins/minerals and crops that may be high in specific nutriments.

Two vegetables contain at least 10 percent of eight vitamins/minerals listed in the U.S. Recommended Daily Allowance (RDA). They are collards and corn. Here are common vegetables ranked

according to the number of nutriments they have in 10 percent or
more of the RDA:

8 nutriments

collards

sweet corn

7 nutriments

peas

kale

parsley

6 nutriments

broccoli

mustard greens

red peppers

5 nutriments

brussel sprouts

New Zealand spinach

spinach

Swiss chard

4 nutriments

green onions

tomatoes

3 nutriments

green beans

cauliflower

potatoes (cooked in skins)

pumpkin

winter squash

green peppers

Some vegetables should also be considerered because they may
be high in specific vitamins or minerals you want to emphasize. Here
are some to consider:

Calcium

collards

kale

mustard greens

Iron

spinach

peas

swiss chard

mustard greens

Vitamin C

peppers

collards

broccoli

brussel sprouts

kale

cauliflower

mustard greens

tomatoes

Vitamin A

carrots

all greens (spinach, collards, kale, New Zealand spinach)

pumpkin

winter squash

broccoli

The prominence of collards and kale in these charts prompted me to experiment with more ways to eat them. Collards and kale may be nutritious, but they are not so readily considered as appealing vegetables. However, I have discovered an appetizing way to prepare these greens. I grow regular Georgia collards and a remarkable purple collard, called tree collard. I also grow plenty of kale. To prepare them, I first boil the leaves for about ten minutes in a small amount of water. With a blender I then grind up the leaves, using the water they were boiled in to save the nutriments. The blended leaves form a deep green puree. Then I prepare a sauce base of some melted margarine and flour and gradually blend in the greens. This pureed kale/collards is delicious in itself or can be enhanced with a sprinkle of parmesan cheese when served. Everyone in our family, including our one-year-old boy, likes collards and kale prepared in this way. Without pureeing, the fibers of the leaves are sometimes tough, though kale has a delightful ruffled appearance. Pureeing in a blender both breaks down the fibers and releases a sweetness that offsets the strong cabbage family taste in the leaves. Broccoli leaves, which are more nutritious than the broccoli head, can also be prepared in this manner.

Sharing Good Vegetables

When you take the time to grow attractive, nutritious, and poison-free vegetables, some moments make it all worthwhile, pushing into the background your occasional battles with aphids or skirmishes with caterpillars. I think of the evening our three-year-old, Karin, after helping me harvest in the garden before dinner, proudly announced over the cauliflower during the meal, as she asked for a second helping, "I picked! I picked!"

I recall another day when the school class of our eleven-year-old, Bart, came to look at the gardens. The children harvested several rich, ripe carrots and cut them into small circles. The cut carrots, so sweet and lush on that May day as we shared the fullness of the garden, seemed like small discs of gold, the quintessential coin of the sun.

5: Grow Your Own Herbs and Fruits

No market produce can compete with the herbs and fruits you grow yourself. Their fresh state and optimum taste make growing them well worth the little trouble required. Your own fresh dill leaves cut up and sprinkled on a salad or your own fresh strawberries picked for dessert will provide memorable eating experiences.

The Basic Herbs

The gourmet in you will quickly assert itself if you have a range of basic herbs at your disposal. In our family, the presence of herbs and hot peppers also makes us less dependent on salt for seasoning. As in growing vegetables, the herb to begin with is the herb you already like. Start with the familiar and proceed outwards. If that herb is parsley, begin with it. It can be used in so many ways that it is difficult to conceive of growing too much parsley.

Herbs take relatively little space and grow well in containers, even quite small containers, so an herb garden should be considered even by the landless apartment dweller. A kitchen window or balcony with herbs in container boxes or pots can be arranged and tended easily. Movable containers are especially good for herbs if you live in a cold climate where the herb can't grow outdoors in winter. Herbs are attractive decorative plants also, featuring the purple flowers of chive and the white blossoms of basil.

I strongly suggest a basic herb garden of six herbs:

basil
chive
dill
oregano
parsley
rosemary

To this list garlic should be added, but I have discussed garlic under vegetables in the onion family. Let me dispatch garlic by saying I eat it almost every day at the evening meal, in melted butter, with basil and oil in a pesto sauce, or as the flavoring to start all top-of-the-stove meat and fish dishes and sauces. Garlic offers so many taste pleasures and has such reputed health value that the maxim "Garlic is as good as ten mothers" may not overstate the case. Garlic has been a favorite taste since the days of the pyramid builders in Egypt. The Greeks called it "the stinking rose," but it is actually in the lily/onion family.

If you want to grow the six basic herbs successfully, here are some questions you'll face:

What is the herb's appearance? The thin spears of chive contrast with the broad shiny leaves of basil. Learning to recognize herbs is not difficult.

What are the herb's seasonal warmth and sunlight requirements? Parsley grows relatively well in cool semishade, but basil benefits from maximum summer sun and warmth.

Is the herb annual or perennial? In mild climates several of these herbs winter over. Chive, oregano, and rosemary grow perpetually in my garden, though I start them new every two years. Dill and basil are annuals. Dill must be sown not merely once but several times during the warm season because it grows quickly to maturity. Parsley can grow more than one season, but I treat it as an annual for best production. Locate perennials where you won't cultivate the soil. With all herbs, a position close to the kitchen is desirable.

What soil is best for herbs? All these herbs like a well-composted but not overly rich soil. Heavy nitrogen in herb soils promotes a lush leaf growth but not a concentration of taste. Herbs also prefer a slightly alkaline soil, so add lime if needed.

What are herb watering requirements? All these herbs like adequate water in a well-drained soil. Especially when it's hot, parsley likes to have a moist soil.

When do you harvest? Harvesting requirements will differ by herb, though the most general rule is that oils are concentrated just before flowers open. All these herbs can be harvested successively, though dill moves quite quickly through its entire cycle. Chive can be snipped at will and puts out new spears. Basil harvests can be prolonged by clipping any white flowers that appear. Rosemary leaves must be removed from the woody stalks.

How will you use herbs? I like all these herbs in melted butter, on salads, in soups, or as a flavoring for meat, fish, and egg dishes. My favorite use of these herbs is in a do-it-yourself salad. Harvest some of your own tender lettuce, tomatoes, and cucumbers. Then arrange on a plate in the center of the table some rough cuttings of all the basic herbs. Make an oil and vinegar dressing without any herbs in it. Then pass a scissors around the table and allow diners to snip the herbs of their choice onto the fresh salad. Your guests who don't have fresh herb gardens will appreciate the unique taste opportunity you can give them.

How will you perpetuate your herb garden? Oregano, rosemary, and chive can be perpetuated vegetatively. Cut a woody stem of oregano or rosemary and root it in moist earth. When my bushes of these two herbs begin to look overgrown, I root new bushes and pull out the old. I separate the clumps of chive and replant them in suitable places. Chive is a perennial in my climate. I start basil, dill, and parsley from seed each spring. The dill keeps dropping seeds and sprouting volunteers from the occasional mature plants that I allow to seed.

What pests can you expect on herbs? Relatively few. In fact, ground-up herbs are sometimes used as an insect deterrent, especially garlic and rosemary. I wash aphids occasionally off declining chive and pick caterpillars from my dill leaves.

How can you store herbs? To extend the peak season production, I freeze all six of these herbs for winter use. I cut, wash, pat dry, and then store them in plastic bags in the freezer. You can dry herbs also. Basil, oregano, and rosemary can be hung in a warm, dry, dark place for three to ten days for best drying. Parsley should be dried quickly in your oven or in a drier for four hours at 160° F. to prevent the green leaves from turning black.

Basil

Basil is a spicy, lush, hot weather annual. Start with seeds or nursery plants in early spring and plant in full sun when assured of warm weather. The plants will grow to a lush foliage on a bush about 2 feet high. This basic herb of Italian cooking also makes an attractive landscape plant for borders. Harvest throughout the growing season, as needed. I use basil with tomato, egg dishes, chicken, and in salads. My favorite basil taste is a pesto sauce (1 cup chopped basil, ⅓ cup olive or lighter salad oil, and 3 large garlic cloves, all pureed in a blender). Use the sauce on pasta, rice, or potatoes.

Chive

Chive is a delicately flavored clumping perennial in the onion family. You can start it from seeds or begin with a clump bought at a nursery. Chive grows well in relatively small containers. The clump can be divided as it grows. Hollow spears of chive thrive in sun or partial shade and like a fairly rich soil for an herb. Keep the soil moist and harvest as needed by cutting individual spears or cutting a

HERB BASIL

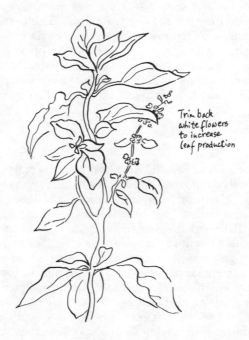

Trim back
white flowers
to increase
leaf production

whole clump an inch above ground level. The clump will regenerate quickly. Aphids must sometimes be washed off chive. I store excess chopped chive by freezing it in small bags. Chive is indispensable over sour cream on potatoes and favored in our house as a topping for cheese and egg dishes. Also a good salad herb.

Dill

Dill is the tallest of these herbs, growing to 3 feet in slender stalks. Dill is an annual, likes full sun, but will grow in partial shade. Feathery dill leaves have a fresh aroma and taste, unlike the intense dry taste of dill seeds. You can gather seeds by letting a plant mature and putting a small paper bag over the seed heads. Secure the bag with a string. Dill grows quickly in warm or cool seasons and re-seeds itself if allowed. Successive plantings during the summer are needed. Begin harvesting as soon as the plant is large enough to survive without the leaf you remove. Dill is excellent in salads, soups, egg dishes, and breads.

Oregano

Oregano is a hearty, small bush that would be sorely missed in our family's salads and sauces if it did not exist. Oregano is not fussy, growing in either full sun or partial shade. This herb takes root easily from cuttings. When my mature plants begin to look tired, I plant a cutting in moist soil to begin a new bush. In my mild winter climate, oregano winters over. I harvest as needed, stripping the small leaves from a woody stalk. This pizza-tasting herb provides an aromatic yet mild taste to tomato dishes, meats, chicken, fish, soups, and salads.

Parsley

Parsley is the all-time favorite herb both because of its clean, crisp taste and its lovely deep green appearance, which serves so well as a garnish. Parsley is high in vitamins A and C and lends taste to all salads, soups, and sauces. This herb freezes well, so you can easily enjoy parsley all through the winter. Parsley makes an attractive low border or an edible bright green landscape plant. Start with seeds in spring. Parsley grows well in cool or hot weather, in full sun or partial shade. Sometimes parsley sprouts with difficulty, so soak the seeds and chill them in the refrigerator if you have difficulty. I don't find sprouting parsley a problem, but the old saying "Parsley seeds must go to the devil and back seven times before sprouting" suggests that some gardeners find parsley sluggish. When growing parsley at home, you can choose from several varieties, including small curly leaf types and larger leaf kinds. Related cilantro has a piquancy favored in Mexican cuisine.

Rosemary

Rosemary is the most dominant of these herbs, a spicy balance for full, rich tastes in meat dishes or wine-simmered fish or chicken. I use it sparingly in salads and more generously in soups. Rosemary's strong taste makes it, fittingly, the herb of remembrance. Crush a leaf between your fingers and the perfume will linger on your hand for hours. Rosemary grows as a low perennial bush but is more sensitive to the cold than oregano and can be started from cuttings only with more attention. Rosemary doesn't like to have its roots get too dry, so keep it well watered. Avoid high-nitrogen fertilizers. Rosemary will winter over in my climate in some years, but not in others. It likes full sun but will grow reasonably well in partial shade. One plant is enough. Harvest by cutting off twigs of rosemary and stripping off the feather-shaped leaves. Like all the herbs, it can be stored for winter use by freezing or drying.

Fruit Growing

Strawberries and dwarf fruit trees can make a big contribution to household fruit production and offer a high-quality taste experience. The reason for better taste is obvious. Market fruit must be picked before its prime so it can ripen in the days from harvest to store, then from purchase to moment of consumption. A red-ripe strawberry pulled right from the plant and eaten is a taste experience of a different and higher order.

Strawberries

Strawberries are my first recommendation for fruit production in a small space garden. I have about two hundred Tioga and Sequoia strawberry plants scattered around my property. They yield two pickings of about 2 pounds each per week from May through October. That's about the right amount of one kind of fruit for our family. Strawberries take little space and grow well in containers. They are nutritious, high in Vitamin C.

Strawberries serve as an attractive green landscape plant with pleasant white flowers and the rich red fruit. Once started, the strawberries increase their numbers with annual runners. In my climate the plants winter over easily. In colder climates a heavy winter mulch of straw is advisable. You can also start from seeds or small plants each spring. I find numerous volunteer strawberry seeds starting out each year. After a plant has produced for two seasons, it grows rather large and bushy, producing less, so I thin the largest plants each season.

Check at local nurseries to find which varieties of strawberries do well in your climate. Some varieties are June bearers, good if you want a big harvest all at once for freezing, canning, or pies. I prefer the long season ever-bearing types.

Keep strawberries well watered and make the soil rich with compost and nutriments. If a strawberry goes dry, the fruit will be inferior. The secret to large, sweet fruits is plenty of water and good sunlight, though I also get a reasonable harvest from my plants in partial shade. When cultivating strawberries, the biggest concern is keeping the fruits off the soil, where they rot quickly with water contact or are susceptible to attacks from slugs or snails. I solve this problem with wire racks, consisting of 1-foot-square pieces of chicken wire with a 3-inch circular center removed and a cut into the center from one side. The four corners are stapled to 2-by-2-by-2-inch scrap wood to elevate the wire. In spring the plants are placed in the wire holders and the fruit develops with no soil contact and fruit loss.

Mulching with pine needles is another good technique to keep

STRAWBERRY HOLDERS

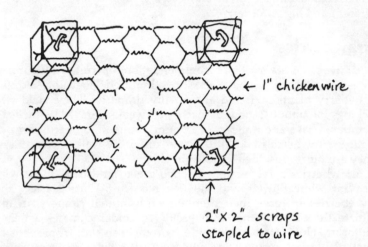

← 1" chicken wire

2" x 2" scraps
stapled to wire

↑ fruits off ground

strawberries off the ground. The pine needles also decompose to make the soil slightly acidic, which strawberries like.

Dwarf Fruit Trees

Dwarf fruit trees should be considered wherever an espalier or border plant might be possible in your edible landscape. Fruit trees are excellent when both ornamentation and food production are desired. The blossoms of my apples are lovely in the spring and the Red and Yellow Delicious apples hang succulently on the branches until eaten in September.

Apples are my favorite, but I also have good luck with dwarf peach, pear, and apricot. Dwarf trees have full-sized fruit but a dwarf rootstock that keeps the tree height anywhere from 6 to 15 feet. In about three years a dwarf tree will bear heavily. My apple trees now produce about 30 pounds of fruit each.

Full-sized fruit trees are desirable only if you have the room and prefer a large crop of one type of fruit rather than a diverse crop of several fruits. I am the fortunate harvester each season of fruit from a full-sized plum tree planted on our property twenty years ago.

When determining what dwarf fruit trees to select and how to plant them, keep the following in mind.

Consider first what kind of fruit you like to eat. Don't start with a persimmon if you've never had one. As with vegetables and herbs, start with the familiar.

Then inquire whether your climate will allow such a species to flourish. The collective growing experience of other gardeners, farmers in your region, local nurserymen, and your county agricultural extension agent can be your guide. Some fruits require winter chilling, which you may or may not have in the right amount. Other fruits require substantial sun and warmth. Oranges grow well in Orange County, California, but not in Minnesota.

Then narrow the choice further to the varieties (within the species) that grow well in your region. For example, there are many kinds of apple trees, but they don't all grow well everywhere. Start with the proven, familiar success stories that local resources can direct you to. Later you may want to send away for more exotic varieties and even start a larger library of grafted trees. Some gardeners have a dozen types of historic and contemporary apples growing on one tree.

When you've narrowed the selection, inquire carefully to determine if the tree needs a pollinizer. Some fruit trees are self-pollinating; others fruit better if a second tree is present.

Buy the fruit trees during the dormant season of winter or early spring. During the dormant period you can buy the trees more cheaply, as trees with bare roots rather than as trees in pots. However, potted trees may be available as a year older, which means earlier fruiting.

When preparing the soil, dig in plenty of composted material and ensure enough nitrogen, phosphorus, and potassium in the soil to give the tree a healthy start. I use compost, manure, rock phosphate or bone meal, and wood ash. Flood the soil well and plant the tree. Stake the young trees with a permanent 2-by-2. When fruit develops, support the branches because dwarf fruit tree branches will break with heavy fruit. Plant on 6- to 8-foot centers, depending on the dwarfing characteristics of the trees you purchased.

In successive years, spray fruit trees during the dormant season with an oil solution that has lime and sulphur in it. Use copper rather than sulphur for apricot trees. These solutions smother overwintering scale insects or aphids and reduce the buildup of fungus and disease in the trees. Aphids are my main fruit tree concern. I wash the aphids off and spread a gummy band of sticky material, trade name Tanglefoot, around the tree to keep ants from getting up in the branches to protect and milk the aphids.

Prune each dormant season to achieve a pleasing symmetry in the tree and to promote growth on strong branches that will support fruit rather than split the trunk. Prune also to make the tree conform to any training plan you may have.

Keep fruit trees well watered and well fed. Compost placed at the base of the tree can be carried to the roots by earthworms. Nutriments can be leached to the roots with water. Dwarf fruit trees can also be grown in containers, but make every effort to supply continuing nutriments with manure tea, fish emulsion, and compost. Water the plants frequently in hot, windy weather to keep them from drying out.

The most painful task annually for the novice fruit tree grower is the pruning of excessive fruits in the spring. Do this when the fruits are the size of marbles. The novice will usually find the cluster of four apples at one location too attractive to prune down to one apple. The results are inevitable. You'll get four smaller and not so sweet apples rather than one large, sweeter apple.

Other Fruits

Other fruit possibilities may be useful in your situation.

Grape vines are attractive landscape plants and good bearers in my backyard. I have some Thompson Seedless and some Black Malukkah. A whole arbor would be possible.

Red currant bushes are also useful edible landscape plants for me, replacing nondescript hedge vegetation.

You may be able to grow various cane berries. If you have children playing in the area, consider berry bushes without thorns, such as thornless loganberries.

Nut trees may also be suitable for your situation. I am fortunate to have a mature almond.

Special trees may flourish in your climate. My microclimate permits avocados.

Full-sized nut trees or an avocado are long-term investments, so plan to be around to enjoy them or present these trees to a future generation.

6: Containers and Community Gardens

We Americans have a luxurious sense of space. When I travel to Europe, especially to the Netherlands, I return home with that impression reinforced. The food producer at the home level in the Netherlands gets a large yield from a small space, a space many American gardeners would consider too small to be productive. In many ways, from the widths of our freeways to our sense of the appropriate size of a house, we are a people of wide open spaces.

Container gardening is an antidotal response to this generous view of space. If you plan to garden in containers, you may have no access to the ground at all. You may live in an apartment or condominium with no ground area. But you can still garden. Or, like me, you may be a homeowner who has run out of ground space. I have about twenty strawberry plants in containers because I needed to create more space than even an efficient use of ground space allowed.

Gardening in containers poses more challenges than gardening in the ground. Exhaust your ground space first and consider the prospect of community gardens, discussed later in this chapter. The structure and fertility of soil in containers must be of high quality because the roots of plants will not have a large reservoir of soil to consider. Container soil can't benefit from a migration of earthworms to aerate it and concentrate nutriments. Watering containers must be watched more carefully than watering in the ground because containers dry out quickly, especially in hot weather when there is wind. Containers should drain quickly or roots will rot. Plant roots can become overheated in containers, but not in the ground.

Containers also have a few distinct advantages. If there is no ground available, of course, they are the route to follow. But containers have one other advantage. They can be moved. As the sun angle changes in the sky, containers can be placed at sunnier locations. When cold weather approaches, containers can sometimes be moved indoors to sheltered, sunny areas. And if you are moving from one dwelling to another, containers are a good way to carry the precious soil you may have worked so hard to create.

CONTAINER GARDENING

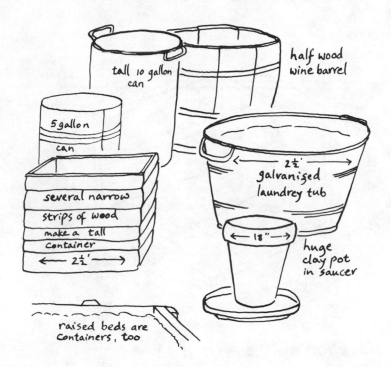

tall 10 gallon can

half wood wine barrel

5 gallon can

2½'
galvanised laundrey tub

several narrow strips of wood make a tall container
← 2½' →

← 18" →

huge clay pot in saucer

raised beds are containers, too

Making Containers

Much attention should be given to the purchase or the proper construction of containers. The first consideration should be size. The larger the better. The minimum size I use is a 1-cubic-foot container. This is a good basic size for many crops, especially shallow-rooted leaf crops, lettuce, and herbs. One cubic foot is also a manageable size to move. I would recommend a 2–4-cubic-foot size for larger plants, such as tomatoes or dwarf fruit trees. The larger the size, the greater opportunity a plant's roots will have to expand. Plant roots in normal soil are longer than you might expect. Beet roots can go down several feet. Also, the larger the size of a container, the greater the reservoir of water from which the plant can draw.

I recommend use of recycled wood for containers. You can find this material under "Lumber, Used" in the Yellow Pages. The cheap-

BUILDING A CONTAINER

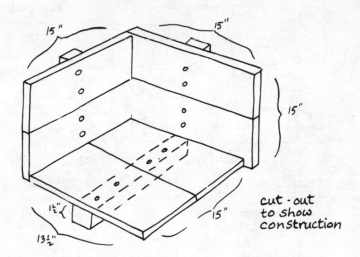

15"

15"

15"

15"

13½"

1½"

cut-out
to show
construction

MATERIALS : 8 pieces of 1"x 8"x 15"
2 pieces of 1"x 8"x 13½"
4 pieces of 2"x 2"x 16½"
1 piece of 2"x 2"x 15"
galvanized nails

the completed
box, planted

1½"

est board available may be 1-by-8. New wood can also be used, but it will be more expensive. Redwood is the ideal lumber because it is so resistant to rot, but redwood is quite expensive. I coat less-durable species with a product of linseed oil and mineral spirits, with some redwood pigment, to preserve my wood and lend some color uniformity to the containers.

I construct a roughly cubic foot container from eight pieces of 1-by-8 board 15 inches long for the sides and two pieces 13½ inches long for the bottom. Four pieces of 2-by-2 that are 16½ inches long support the sides and keep the container slightly raised off the ground for drainage. A 15-inch 2-by-2 on the bottom adds stability. I always use hot dipped galvanized nails that won't rust readily.

Wood has several virtues as a container material. You can drill holes in it easily. You can make wood containers to any dimension. When building a climbing rack for some crops (tomatoes, cucumbers, beans, peas), you can nail the rack to the outside of a wood container rather than occupy valuable root space inside the container. And if strong winds are a factor in your location, several wood containers can be nailed together with a long 2-by-2 to give each other added stability.

Old wine and whiskey barrels, cut in half, also make good containers, especially for potatoes, tomatoes, squash, and dwarf fruit trees. Discarded round cardboard ice cream containers, often available free from ice cream stores, make excellent containers for one season.

Red clay pots can be purchased and make good containers, but they are usually rather small. Clay has one advantage over plastic: It breathes and allows moisture to escape from the pot. Plastic does not, which makes drainage at the bottom more critical to avoid root rot. Pressed paper pots are another desirable container material, especially if you later want to establish the plant, such as a dwarf fruit tree, in the ground. You can then plant the entire paper pot without disturbing roots, but cut off the bottom of the planter and slit the sides so the roots can expand freely.

Container Soil

Container soil must be high in nutriments, constantly replenished with nutriments, and able to absorb moisture but drain readily.

Well-made compost makes a good container soil. (A mix of one-third garden soil and two-thirds compost also works well for me.) If you don't have that much compost, you can make your own container soil by mixing one part sand (river sand, not salty ocean sand), one part garden soil or good topsoil, and one part loose organic material (peat moss, leaf mold, ground bark, aged sawdust). You can ensure this soil will be free of pests and diseases by dumping it into a pan of water and heating the pan on an outdoor barbecue at 180° F. for one hour. The smell may be pungent. Sterilization of the soil in this manner is not crucial but can sometimes be helpful if your soil has much fungus and wilt disease.

You can buy container soil in bags from nurseries. Buy in as large a bulk as possible to get the best price. Consider making all your containers and then buying a cubic yard of container soil from a nursery.

Lightweight potting soil mixes, sometimes referred to as University of California or Cornell mixes, are also good container soil. These mixes are combinations of mineral material (sand or vermiculite) and organic material (peat moss). The mixtures have a unique ability to absorb large amounts of moisture. Their light weight can be advantageous if you have to move containers or have a balcony/ rooftop location where weight is a factor. Lightweight containers need added protection against wind blowing them over.

Potting soil mixes, like all container soil, require periodic addition of nutriments. I use manure tea, sometimes made from bought chicken or cow manure. Put some manure in a cloth or fiberglass bag, steep it in a 5-gallon pail, then dilute to a light brown and ladle the tea onto the container soil. Liquid fish emulsion or kelp liquid nutriments are convenient for container fertility. A side dressing of compost continues to improve soil structure in containers. Watering will leach down nutriments in the compost.

Watering Containers

Monitor your containers carefully in hot weather to be sure they receive and drain water properly. A 1-cubic-foot container outdoors in hot and windy summer weather may require two waterings per day. Drainage must also be rapid in containers or the roots can rot. I drill the bottoms of my containers with 1-inch augers 6 inches on center. Then I cover the inside bottom of the container with a fine mesh fiberglass screen, stapling the edges.

When watering your containers, you'll gradually learn to weigh all the variables: heat, amount of direct sunlight, wind, container size, speed of soil drainage, and water requirements of the given plant. Squash and tomatoes require ample water deep into the container. Lettuce requires constant water in the top inches for its shallow roots.

While watering, inspect to be sure the water actually penetrates the roots. Sometimes containers dry and the soil shrinks, pulling away from the side. The water runs down the sides, between the soil and the container, and out the drainhole, without actually penetrating the roots. If this happens, it's a good idea to set the container in a large tub of water and saturate the soil. When no more bubbles arise, the soil is saturated. Take the container out and let it drain.

Drip irrigation systems are particularly good for containers because they emit small amounts of water over a long time. Little water is wasted in runoff and the danger of containers drying rapidly is diminished. Soft container soil can be easily washed out with normal hose watering.

When planting in containers, be careful not to overcrowd. Imagine the size of mature plants and then allow them the same space you would in the ground. However, plants at the edges of containers can use some of the area beyond the container for their sun catching.

When planting seedlings in a container, follow the same directions as for ground planting. However, when thinning seedlings in a container, cut the plants rather than pull them out if the soil is quite soft and if other adjacent plants have roots that might be disturbed.

Containers can produce plentiful harvests where no ground access is possible.

Container Plants

When choosing vegetables, herbs, and fruit for container gardening, choose a plant whose root system will develop adequately in the size of container you have.

All herbs and leaf vegetables will grow well in 1-cubic-foot containers. For maximum production I suggest leaf lettuce and cut-and-come-again leafy greens (chard, collards, kale, New Zealand spinach). Long-fruiting plants, such as zucchini or tomato, in 2-cubic-foot containers would be my second recommendation. Salad onions, herbs, and root crops can also grow well in containers. Strawberries and dwarf fruit trees are good container choices.

You can grow either full-sized plants or specially developed miniature plants bred for container production. The major seed catalogs will feature varieties specially suggested for containers. Here are some to try:

bush beans: Tendercrop
beets: Little Egypt
carrots: Little Finger
corn: Faribo Golden Midget
cucumber: Patio Pick
eggplant: Modern Midget

lettuce: Tom Thumb
melons: New Hampshire Midget
peas: Little Marvel
squash: Scaloppine
tomato: Tiny Tim

Community Gardens

For the gardener without a growing space, there is another option besides containers: a community garden, a shared ground away from your living site. About two million Americans now participate in some kind of community garden program. According to a recent Gallop survey on gardening, another seven million households responded that someone in the household would like to food garden if space were available.

Community gardens have one strong advantage over home-site gardening: They provide a constant exchange of information and camaraderie among gardeners. Your food-growing education can progress faster in a community garden than in the isolation of your home site. The supportive group of fellow food gardeners can encourage you in gardening and lead to the development of friendships with like-minded people.

There may already be some community gardens going in your community. Investigate this. Massachusetts has been a leading state, allotting public park space for community gardens. There are forty-five community gardens going now in San Francisco. A national organization promoting food gardening can assist you in efforts to locate or organize community gardens. Contact Gardens for All (see Chapter 8).

Local municipal governments, park and recreation departments, schools, churches, civic groups, garden clubs, and private corporations are all potential sponsors of community gardens. For example, alongside the Palo Alto, California, public library there are now spaces for about two hundred food gardeners. The city furnishes the land and free water as part of its parks and open space service to its people. Citizens are assured they can keep their plots as long as they actively garden them. All gardening takes place within an organic strategy, with group composting piles and plenty of compost available to enrich beds. "We have another 180 people on the waiting list," says garden coordinator Pat Reposo. "We're looking for more space."

When setting up a community garden, she counsels, the best land strategy is situating the garden within the protective domain of a park. The frustrating results of setting up community gardens on temporarily donated land are apparent in Palo Alto, where an active community gardening organization, called Ecology Action, set up a several-acre garden on land donated by the Syntex Corporation. John Jeavons, the energetic and visionary director of Ecology Action, worked from 1972 to 1980 on this land to develop the soil and perform quantifiable, rigorous tests to show the productivity of organic gardening or farming, digging deep the beds with organic material. Unfortunately, Syntex expanded and decided they needed to use the land for a parking lot, which set back this research by several years. The incentive to develop soil will be greatest if you either own the land or are assured it won't be withdrawn from food gardening.

7: Control Insects, Disease, and Weeds

Growing food in an urban area is in many respects easier than doing so in a rural region. That's because in the country your vegetables are attractive to deer, raccoons, gophers, moles, and birds in large numbers. In an urban area there are usually fewer of these competitors around. The quantity of insects to be regarded as possible competitors is also greater in a rural area.

In an urban area, however, you have more dogs and cats to contend with. I've found they can usually be kept out of the vegetable area with physical barriers, such as gates, and with raised beds that show them where to walk.

In all vegetable gardening, however, there are competing insects, debilitating plant diseases, and vigorous competing plants (weeds) to contend with.

Control Insects

A pest is an insect in the wrong place, at the wrong time, and in too great a number. Insects should not be regarded as evil. The garden can become a satisfying zoo of small wildlife whose diversity and beauty are impressive. Pest is a harsh word. The ants that are troublesome do wonderful service cleaning up the slugs and snails you kill. Flies that are problems also assist in pollinating. Always aim to control, not dominate, the insect population. Pest and predator insects must continue to survive if they are to maintain each other in equilibrium. Keep nature's balance, but shift the balance slightly in your favor.

In my urban vegetable garden I have minor, acceptable insect damage without the use of any pesticides. The opportunity to grow vegetables without pesticides is one of the appeals of urban gardening. The clear and present danger to human health and to wildlife from pesticides and herbicides has been amply documented. It should also be noted that pesticides don't work for the food producer in the long run. Thirty years ago American farmers were using fifty million pounds of pesticides per year and losing 7 percent of their crops to insect pests. Now they are using six hundred million pounds per year and are losing about twice the percentage of crops.

Pesticides tend to kill predators as well as pest insects. The pests become resurgent and resistant. Secondary insects, not formerly pests, step into wastelands created by pesticides and become pests. One of the saddest effects of pesticides is that they tend to kill pollinators, especially the bees, without which most vegetable reproduction would be impossible.

Here are the steps to follow to garden successfully, as I do, without any toxic pesticides.

1. When you see damage, learn to identify the cause. The cause is not always obvious. Your mowed-off seedlings may have been eaten by birds rather than snails. Damage to a broccoli leaf may have been caused by slugs or caterpillars. Identifying the life cycle of pest insects is a crucial first step. When the white cabbage moths are flying, be prepared to handle their caterpillar offspring.

Also learn to identify the main predator insects that assist you. Ladybugs eat many aphids. Lacewings and their larvae are the most beneficial allies you have. Small wasps also help by being parasitic to moth larvae.

2. Modify habitats to reduce pest damage. Snails and slugs can be restrained in an uneasy truce but never really controlled if you keep that large ivy hedge to which they retreat. Eliminate all hospitable homes for pests.

3. Tolerate some damage. Realize that plants are strong. When beyond the seedling stage, plants can withstand relatively large amounts of leaf damage and still produce abundantly. The ability of plants to recover and regenerate should not be underestimated.

4. Begin with physical barriers. Sawdust or ashes around plants or along pathways between beds will stop migrating slugs and snails, which don't like to expose their mucous membranes to such abrasive materials. Ashes also deter the maggots that damage root crops. Bands of camphor gum, trade name Tanglefoot, effectively prevent ants from climbing fruit trees to "milk" aphids and protect them from their enemies. Mineral oil on the silk of a corn cob can prevent borer attacks. Collars around seedlings protect against cutworms. Tarpaper squares around cabbage family stalks prevent flies from laying eggs that become root maggots. Nets over tender seedlings can keep birds off. Wrens are insect eaters, but many other birds eat both insects and small plants. I protect my strawberries from slugs with the 1-foot-square racks of chicken wire described in "Strawberries" in Chapter 5. I cut a circular center out of the wire for the plant and elevate the four corners by stapling on scraps of lumber 2-by-2-by-2.

5. Increase the predator insects. Do this in two ways. First, make your garden hospitable to known predators. When you see a ladybug, make sure it is not destroyed. Ladybug larvae can eat twenty

BENEFICIAL INSECTS

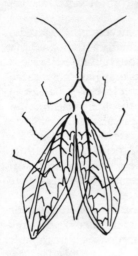

Lacewing

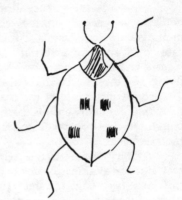

Ladybug

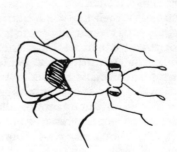

Trichogramma Wasp
(magnified)

aphids per hour. The adult ladybug is a less-voracious feeder. Learn to identify the larvae of lacewings, which eat many aphids and other competing insects. Keep flowering plants going as constantly as possible to provide nectar for the small wasps that are parasites on some pest insects. The Compositae family flowers, such as calendulas and sunflowers, are especially helpful because they have so many pollen sources on one flower head. You may also elect to import additional ladybugs, lacewings, and miniature trichogramma wasps or syrphid flies. Write the biological supply houses listed in Chapter 8 or consult your local nursery, if it carries these forward-looking control methods.

6. Coordinate your watering for good pest control. Slugs and snails like moist nighttime environments. You may want to water in the morning rather than the evening at times when these pests are active.

7. Hand pick. I reduce snail, slug, and cabbage caterpillar populations on five-minute midnight patrols whenever their numbers increase.

8. Use fine, powerful mists from a hose nozzle to dislodge aphids and whitefly buildups. A fine spray from a nozzle is probably my most effective single method of pest control. Moving through the garden, I use such a spray to dislodge small colonies of aphids, wash off caterpillars, and disrupt whitefly populations. The populations of these pests can become sufficiently disrupted that the plant surges ahead, perhaps to harvest, before the problem arises again. Moving through the garden, using my left hand as guide among the leaves and my right hand as holder of the fine, powerful nozzle spray, I can monitor and disrupt pest activity.

9. Use the botanical spore, Bacillus thuringiensis (BT), on caterpillars where there is a major hatch of moth larvae. Sold under the trade names Dipel, Biotrol, and Thuricide, this spore comes as a powder and is mixed 1 tablespoon to a gallon of water. Bacillus thuringiensis disrupts caterpillar digestion, eventually causing death, but is safe to other species of animals. This is a good example of tilting a natural control in your direction. I use BT once a week on my cabbage family crops when the moths are flying. Also good on tomato hornworms. Crisp fall weather eventually inhibits the life cycles of moths.

10. Spray fruit trees in the dormant season with oil, lime, and sulphur mixes, applied with water. The oil suffocates mites, scale insects, and aphids that winter over. Sulphur is a valuable reducer of fungus disease. Apricot trees don't like to be sulphured, however. Use copper and oil on them.

11. Improve your soil fertility to grow plants quickly. Fast-growing, healthy plants are an important natural deterrent against insect pests. Weak, old, stressed plants tend to be attractive to pests. The faster you can grow your vegetables, the less the pests will be a concern.

12. Diversify your plantings to reduce pest damage. In my garden the natural flow of the crops, one following another in whatever space is available, precludes large monoculture blocks of plants. Monocultures are unstable in proportion to their size. A small home garden can be sufficiently diversified that pests have a difficult time expanding their territory, even if they vanquish one plant. Strong-smelling herbs and flowers can disrupt the homing power of insects. Marigold roots exude a secretion that repels some nematodes, small, thready worms that retard plant growth.

13. Keep the season on your side. If you have a major pest in your situation, consider when its life cycle will be active. If the larvae of flies, in the heat of summer, damage your carrots and radishes, spread ashes around the plants. If that fails, try growing carrots and radishes in the cool season rather than at the height of summer.

14. Plant mature seedlings. The greatest danger to vegetables is in the immediate period after the seed sprouts and while it attains a few inches of height. At this time birds, snails, and slugs do their damage. I raise as many plants as possible in pest-proof seed boxes and then set the plants out when they have the strength and size to survive any damage that might occur. Raising seedlings to set out, rather than putting space into seeds, also makes best use of the small space.

To review, manage the most common insect attackers with the numbered techniques outlined, as follows:

ants: 1, 3, 4, 8, 10
aphids, whiteflies: 1, 3, 4, 5, 8, 10, 11, 12, 13
caterpillars: 1, 3, 5, 7, 8, 9, 11, 12
beetles: 1, 3, 7, 11, 12
slugs: 1, 2, 3, 4, 6, 7, 11, 12, 14
snails: 1, 2, 3, 4, 6, 7, 11, 12, 14
root maggots: 1, 3, 4, 5, 11, 12, 13
cutworms: 1, 4, 5, 7, 9, 11, 12, 14

Plant Diseases

A healthy soil is your first line of defense against plant diseases. Grow plants quickly and harvest them before they decline.

Four other main preventive measures can be taken if disease becomes a problem. First, water in a manner that keeps diseases

AN INSECT- RESISTING VEGETABLE

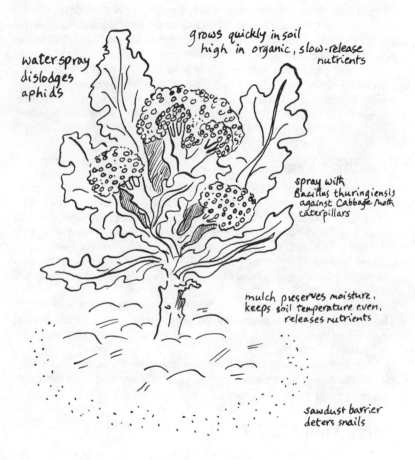

water spray dislodges aphids

grows quickly in soil high in organic, slow-release nutrients

spray with Bacillus thuringiensis against Cabbage Moth caterpillars

mulch preserves moisture, keeps soil temperature even, releases nutrients

sawdust barrier deters snails

BROCCOLI

down. Mildew is a common way for squash, tomatoes, beans, and peas to die. If you water the leaves of these plants, especially in the evening, allowing water to remain on the leaves throughout the night, the plants will eventually succumb to mildew. The young plants are relatively immune, but older plants with developed leaves will mildew. If you harvest plants when leaves are wet, you also help transmit disease. Solution: Rather than spray, bubble water onto the ground over the plant root; harvest when the leaves are dry.

Second, rotate your crops. This is a basic technique for reducing the buildup of wilts and other plant diseases in your soil. Move the plants on successive seasons and years.

Third, if you have a wilt problem with tomatoes and other crops, select wilt-resistant varieties. Tomatoes with VF on the seed packet means that this tomato is resistant to verticillium and fusarium wilt.

Fourth, spray dormant fruit trees to keep down disease buildup, such as peach leaf curl.

Minimize Weeds

Once they've sprouted, weeds have never been known to grow smaller. Five minutes of weeding maintenance per day is better than an hour on Saturday. Monitor your garden carefully and remove young weeds. Weeds benefit the garden by concentrating minerals in their green bodies. The minerals can then be recycled back through the compost pile and into the garden. Learn to make compost skillfully so it will heat up to 160° F. for a long period to kill weed seeds.

Space your plantings so the leaves of mature plants just touch. This umbrella will assist you by keeping out the sunlight that weeds need. The shade will also keep the soil moist and the soil temperature stable.

Mulches are also helpful for reducing weeds. Leaves, lawn clippings, sawdust, and other materials can be spread around maturing plants to keep down the weeds.

Enjoy Your Garden

If you follow the instructions and example of this book, you can become a successful small space vegetable gardener. You can provide tasty poison-free food in great variety for yourself and your family. You can produce this food while improving your soil rather than participate in a system that provides your food while sometimes destroying the soil. In food gardening, you will also gain valuable, satisfying knowledge from your own experience, as opposed to the many derived knowledges that we learn through secondary experiences, such as watching TV. The shared experience of parent and child growing vegetables together can be a memory for both to treasure.

Food-gardening knowledge is an accumulated wisdom joining you to your local comrades and to all food-producing forebearers going back to the first people who planted crops. You can join hands with them through time. When growing your own food, you gain control over one more aspect of your life, and from that plateau you may be able to direct your life further rather than let it be directed by others or by events. As an on-site producer, you are making a major contribution to the overall energy picture by reducing the vast amounts of oil needed every day to produce and distribute foods grown commercially. This saving of depletable energy sources is one of your legacies to future generations.

In a household garden developed with the techniques I have described, you can establish a sustainable agriculture for you and your family that can continue for generations to come, with little energy input, with no need for pesticides, and with a constant improvement of the soil. In food gardening you can combine the benefits of economy with the most exalted experiences of the gourmet. Eating your own food will bring you as close to a sacramental act as you are likely to experience in this secular society. Best of all, the results of food gardening can be shared. The fulfillment and pleasure radiates out to all those with whom you share a meal.

8: Resources for the Food Gardener

Seed Catalogs

For much information on vegetables, for gardener encouragement on long winter nights, and for dreaming of future harvests, seed catalogs are a wonderful resource. Seed companies usually send them free to prospective gardeners.

W. Atlee Burpee Co.
6350 Rutland Ave.
Riverside, CA 92502

DeGiorgio Co.
Council Bluffs, IA 51502

Farmer's Seed and Nursery Co.
Fairibault, MN 55021

Gurney Seed and Nursery Co.
1448 Page St.
Yankton, SD 57078

Joseph Harris Co.
Moreton Farm
Rochester, NY 14624

J. L. Hudson Seed Co.
Box 1058
Redwood City, CA 94064

Jackson and Perkins
Medford, OR 97501

Nichols Garden Nursery
1190 N. Pacific Highway
Albany, OR 97321

George W. Park Seed Co.
Box 31
Greenwood, SC 29647

Stokes Seeds
Box 548
Buffalo, NY 14240

Tsong and Ma International
1556 Laurel St.
San Carlos, CA 94070

Government Information

One of the best investments of your tax dollars has been your county's Cooperative Extension Service, a joint effort of your state universities, federal government financing, and county government assistance. Look in your phone book under "County Offices, Agricultural Extension."

The extension agents can assist you with specific free information about all your food-growing concerns. The great strength of the extension system is its county or state approach, geared to your region. An extension agent has knowledge about local soils, local pH, what kinds of vegetables thrive in your climate, and how you can use biological controls against pests and disease. Some extension agents act as plant pathologists to help you troubleshoot any problems. Your extension agent can offer you a range of free literature.

For example, at a visit to the Hayward, California, office of my Alameda County extension agent, Kathy Hesketh, I received an informative forty-page booklet, *Home Vegetable Gardening*, plus several shorter pamphlets: *What, Where and How to Plant; Planning and Preparing the Vegetable Garden; Vegetable Planting Without Weeds; Planting and Harvesting Times in California; Raised Bed Vegetables;* and *Controlling Insects and Disease in the Home Garden.*

Your local extension agent will offer similar literature, which is generally of high quality, providing the collective local wisdom of generations of food growers in your climate area.

There may also be other extension personnel at your disposal. Available for questions in my county are a soils advisor, a poultry and rabbits advisor for the home food producer who wants to add these systems to vegetable production, and a home economist, available for free telephone consulting and literature on canning, freezing, and drying home produce.

You've paid for these services with your taxes, so take advantage of them as good local information sources. I've found the extension people are courteous and like to help out. You may find them strong partisan enthusiasts for the home food gardening "movement." Kathy Hesketh, for example, heads an ambitious master gardener education program of free classes to teach home food production.

The federal government also has several good gardening brochures, most of which are free. This federal literature is similar to what your local extension service publishes, but with nationwide application, so the data will be less attuned to your local climate. Write for a free list of these brochures to Consumer Information Center, Department Y, Pueblo, Colorado 81009 or to Superintendent of Documents, U.S. Government Printing Office, Washington, D.C. 20402. Government Printing Office bookstores in 20 major cities also stock this literature. Ask for the list of home and garden bulletins. Here are some of the food-gardening brochures you can specifically request along with the list:

Home Garden Vegetables, #671F
Growing Vegetables in the Home Garden. #202
Minigardens for Vegetables, #163
Growing Tomatoes in the Home Garden, #074F
Growing Vegetables in Containers, #669F
Herbs, #670F
Fruits and Nuts, #668F
Organic Gardening—Think Mulch, #672F
Controlling Insects on Fruit and Nut Trees without Insecticides, #072F

Community Food Gardens Movement

Gardens For All, 180 Flynn Ave., Burlington, VT 05401 (802–863–1308) is a nonprofit organization that promotes home food gardening and the efforts of landless urban people to develop community gardens. If you write or phone them, they can alert you to community gardens that may exist in your area. Their files cover such gardens in over two thousand towns and cities. Gardens For All can send you, for $1, their forty-page booklet, *Your Independence Garden for the 80's.* They'll also assist you if you want to start a community food garden.

Here is a partial list of cities with active food gardening programs providing space for urban people who don't have land. I include the list just to give you some sense of the national scope of this movement, which now includes two million Americans in community gardens:

East: New York, Boston, Hartford, Syracuse, Newark, Philadelphia, and Harrisburg

Midwest: Ann Arbor, Detroit, Cleveland, Columbus, Dayton, Indianapolis, Chicago, Milwaukee, Minneapolis, and Kansas City

South: Atlanta, Louisville, St. Louis, and Houston

West: Seattle, Portland, Eugene, Sacramento, San Francisco, San Jose, Santa Barbara, Los Angeles, and Denver

Magazines and Books

Several publishing centers have arisen as suppliers of food-gardening literature. Send a stamped, self-addressed envelope to get a list of their resources. Among them:

Rodale Press, 33 E. Minor, Emmaus, PA 18049. Their monthly magazine, Organic Gardening, *is a useful resource. The Rodale Press also has many books on various food growing subjects. Write for a catalog.*

Family Food Garden *is a monthly magazine published at 1999 Shephard Rd., St. Paul, MN 55116. Another good continuing source of home food-gardening information.*

Garden Way, Charlotte, VT 05445, publishes books and pamphlets on food-gardening subjects. Write for a catalog.

Mother Earth News, *Box 70, Hendersonville, NC 28739, publishes many specialized pamphlets on aspects of food gardening. Write for a catalog.*

For a general checklist of the best available food-gardening books on various subjects, write to Ecology Action/Common Ground, 2225 El Camino Real, Palo Alto, CA 94306. You can order the books from them by mail.

Supplies

If biological controls are not easily available in your area, write direct to major suppliers. Bacillus thuringiensis is an invaluable control for caterpillars on cabbage family plants and other crops. Probably you can find this at local garden stores under the trade names Dipel, Biotrol, or Thuricide. Control insects may be more difficult for you to find locally. Lacewing larvae and trichogramma wasps are the most effective first insect control to recommend. Ladybugs can also be useful for aphid and mite control. The two supply houses listed below can also provide more specialized controls, such as aphitis wasps for red scale insects. To get a brochure about their resources and a list of prices, send a stamped, self-addressed envelope to

Rincon Vitova Insectaries
PO Box 95
Oak View, CA 93022

California Green Lacewings
54 South Bear Creek Drive
Merced, CA 95340

For a good catalog of quality hand tools, from watering cans to trowels, send 50 cents to

Walter F. Nicke
Box 667G
Hudson, NY 12534

If you want a sophisticated soil test kit and can't find one in your area, write to

LaMotte Kit
Box 329
Chestertown, MD 21620